Smart Guide™
to
Relieving Stress

About Smart Guides™

Welcome to Smart Guides. Each Smart Guide is created as a written conversation with a learned friend; a skilled and knowledgeable author guides you through the basics of the subject, selecting the most important points and skipping over anything that's not essential. Along the way, you'll also find smart inside tips and strategies that distinguish this from other books on the topic.

Within each chapter you'll find a number of recurring features to help you find your way through the information and put it to work for you. Here are the user-friendly elements you'll encounter and what they mean:

The Keys

Each chapter opens by highlighting in overview style the most important concepts in the pages that follow.

Smart Moves

Here's where you will learn opinions and recommendations from experts and professionals in the field.

Street Smarts

This feature presents smart ways in which people have dealt with related issues and shares their secrets for success.

Smart Sources

Each of these sidebars points the way to more and authoritative information on the topic, from organizations, corporations, publications, Web sites, and more.

Smart Definition

Terminology and key concepts essential to your mastering the subject matter are clearly explained in this feature.

F.Y.I.

Related facts, statistics, and quick points of interest are noted here.

What Matters, What Doesn't

Part of learning something new involves distinguishing the most relevant information from conventional wisdom or myth. This feature helps focus your attention on what really matters.

The Bottom Line

The conclusion to each chapter, here is where the lessons learned in each section are summarized so you can revisit the most essential information of the text.

One of the main objectives of the *Smart Guide to Relieving Stress* is not only to help you pinpoint those things that are causing you stress but also to better inform you how to deal with all manner of stress so that you can live a more productive, happy, and fuller life.

Smart Guide™

to

Relieving Stress

Carole Bodger

CADER BOOKS

John Wiley & Sons, Inc.

New York • Chichester • Weinheim • Brisbane • Singapore • Toronto

"Life Changes Questionnaire" on pages 31–34 is reprinted from *Journal of Psychosomatic Research,* volume 43, issue 3, pages 272–92, Mark A. Miller and Richard H. Rahe, "Life Changes Scaling for the 1990s," copyright 1997, with permission from Elsevier Science.

The information contained in this book is not intended to serve as a replacement for professional medical advice. Any use of the information in this book is at the reader's discretion. The author and the publisher specifically disclaim any and all liability arising directly or indirectly from the use or application of any information contained in this book. A health-care professional should be consulted regarding your specific situation.

ISBN 0-471-31858-2

Printed in the United States of America

10 9 8 7 6 5 4 3 2 1

To my husband,
Edwin Bon

Acknowledgments

The number of people involved in the creation of this book, as all others, goes far beyond the one name that appears on its cover. To acknowledge each one individually would far exceed our allocated page, but to the many who shared their knowledge, time, and experience, I give my most sincere thanks. Special gratitude is due Robert S. Benchley, for his continuing friendship and support; Rosalind Bodger, Haydee and José Bon, Nancy Feigen, Chris Mackay, and Susan Thor, whose encouragement helped lower my stress levels chapter by chapter; Steven Ricci, who managed to make me laugh even on deadline; and the editorial staff of John Wiley & Sons and Cader Books, notably Michael Cader, Heather Jackson, and John Jusino, the best antidotes to anxiety an author could hope to have. Most of all, to the Lord, and to my husband, Ed Bon, whose love soothes my every stress into blissful serenity, I am indebted.

—C.B.

Atlanta, September 1998

Contents

Introduction

I had just left my job, relocated to a new state, gotten married, bought a new house, and was moving into it when I was invited to write a book about stress relief. On deadline. No better research scenario could have been devised to test the advice we'd share.

Our findings: stress-management techniques do work. Whether you're under the pressure of major life changes, facing a particularly hectic season at work, or simply struggling for day-to-day survival in today's increasingly high-pressure world, you can lessen your anxiety, along with its negative impact on your life. And in the pages ahead we hope to show you how.

We start by looking at what exactly stress is, how we emotionally and physically experience it, how our way of life makes us more likely to encounter it, and the far-ranging effects it can have on both body and mind. In chapters 2 and 3 we examine the many varieties of anxiety—and where we find them—to learn which ones we as individuals are most susceptible to, and so how to best lessen or avert their particular effects. We might expect to be troubled by changes for the worse, but all life transitions, even those that are joyous, can present hardships along the way. Chapter 4 reveals how and why what can make us happy can also leave us so stressed.

The second half of this book presents anxiety-relieving strategies and solutions, beginning with some practical ways in which we can cut back on the sheer number of stressors in our lives—both external and self-imposed. If we can eliminate the existence of a problem, in other words, no problem. We move on, in chapter 6, to the emotional and spiritual defenses we can muster to lessen the impact of our troubles, including the naturally calming and healthful benefits of laughter and tears, meditation and prayer. If we can stop experiencing something as a problem, in other words, no problem.

Neither can physical health be overlooked. Smart lifestyle choices—a nutritious diet, adequate rest, and moderate physical activity—provide a solid foundation for serenity, helping us not only to experience less stress, but also to better cope with it when it does appear.

We conclude by examining some of the pleasurable ways in which we can break the cycle of worry by turning our bodies, minds, and attention to positive, affirming pursuits—from surrounding ourselves with calming music and images and pampering ourselves to lending a hand toward making our world a better, more peaceful place.

We wish we could promise this book as an antidote to all anxiety. We cannot. To those who, after reading it, find their nerves occasionally flaring, a tension headache brewing, or other signs and symptoms of stress still evident in their lives, we say, "Welcome to the human condition." None of us is immune. But while we may not be able to eradicate stress entirely from our existence, if we learn to reduce its frequency of occurrence, to increase our ability to cope with it, and to stop stressing about the fact that we surely will be stressed from time to time, we will succeed in lessening its toll.

....

CHAPTER 1

What Is Stress?

THE KEYS

• The formula for measuring stress—its causes, its effects, and whether we view it in a positive or negative light—is as individual as we are.

• Designed to protect us from real or perceived threats, the "stress response" can become a threat in itself if sustained for extended periods of time.

• Numerous diseases and physical maladies can be caused or exacerbated by emotional duress.

• From the emotional depth of memory to the logic behind our systems of thought, stress can transform the mind.

• The technology intended to make our lives easier is overwhelming today's world with anxiety-producing levels of information.

Take a deep breath. Slowly exhale. Now do it again.

A book about stress relief is a little like stress itself: it might start out by giving you a few butterflies in the stomach, but if it does what it should, it will heighten your senses and ready you for action, and by the time you've finished reading it, it will have brought you to a calmer, safer place. Unlike stress, this book will help you arrive at that place by choice.

Stress Defined

Stress. Why, just the word alone can send tremors up our spines, get our hearts racing and our lungs working harder, and cause any one of the numerous signs that show we're under a lot of pressure. What we commonly called "nerves," "anxiety," and "tension," we now sum up in one nasty, six-letter word that seems to come at us wherever we turn.

Round-the-clock news programs warn us of catastrophes in every corner of the world, crimes across the country, plagues in the laboratory, and health hazards in our own homes. Super computers and fax machines barrage us with information, beepers beep us on our days off, cell phones ring in our cars. In a day and age when more work is demanded for less pay, job security is but a fond memory, family and friends cry out for quality time, parents compete for the "right" nursery schools for their children, and our leisure time is endangered by the pressure we feel to enjoy it, stress is a fact of life. It almost seems that if we're not stressed, we must not be alive.

Some people do seem to thrive on it. You know the type: people who don't start writing that report until they're in danger of losing their job; people who don't stop smoking until a suspicious shadow shows on an X-ray; or people who get all their Christmas shopping done in one fell swoop— on Christmas Eve. One person's stress is another person's motivation.

Others of us, when faced with the life changes, the demands upon our time or resources, and the various trials and tribulations from which stress springs, become deer in the headlights. Paralyzed. Frozen. Overwhelmed.

Whether *acute* (prompted by a specific event) or *chronic* (due to an accumulation of day-to-day anxieties), stress can eat away at us. Even if we are the types for whom stressful situations are motivating, while we may seem to be benefitting (as far as getting things done), on a sustained basis we may still be doing our bodies harm.

Stress comes from a variety of sources—worries about situations beyond our control; fears of illness or financial ruin; concerns about not making it to an appointment on time; even concern over a bad hair day when a big date is planned, to name just a few. The important thing to note is that in many cases stress can have less to do with the event or situation itself than with our perception of what that event or situation means. We have a strong say in determining the impact of stress on our daily lives.

Some of the causes of stress and factors that influence stress' effects on us are unavoidable, and knowing what they are and how they work can lessen their strength. Others can be changed, and in the process radically reduce both stress and its negative impact on our lives. That's why you're reading this book.

SMART SOURCES

National Institute of
  Mental Health
5600 Fishers Lane
  Room 7C-02
Rockville, MD 20857
888-8-ANXIETY
800-64-PANIC
www.nimh.nih.gov

NIMH provides a wealth of public information about panic and anxiety disorders and how to differentiate them from common stress. Call its toll-free information lines, explore its panic and anxiety Web sites, or write to receive free information.

Panic:
www.nimh.nih.gov/
publicat/upd.htm

Anxiety:
www.nimh.nih.gov/
publicat/anxiety.htm

SMART DEFINITION

Stress response

A commonly used term for the body's hormonal reaction to protect itself against real or perceived threats, also sometimes referred to as the "fight or flight" response. A healthy bodily mechanism, the stress response can become overused, leaving the body always on "alert," when stress is sustained for extended periods of time.

Who Needs Stress?

Just like all of our bodies' parts and perceptions, feelings of stress exist for a reason.

Bodily changes involved in what has come to be known as the *stress response* enable us to react in ways—and at levels—that would otherwise be impossible, helping us to defend ourselves from danger of many kinds and allowing us to accomplish what we might not be able to under ordinary circumstances. At the sight of a wild animal ready to pounce, surges of hormones would course through the bodies of our ancestors who, with hearts pounding, would be able to run away faster—and for a longer period of time—than they otherwise would have been able to do. Those tales of mothers able to single-handedly lift automobiles off their trapped children are other examples of the positive power of the stress response.

Like most unpleasant feelings that we experience, stress also serves as an alarm. Much as the gas company adds a noticeable scent to dangerous but odorless vapors to let us detect a problem that might otherwise go unrecognized, our body sends uncomfortable feelings as a signal that something needs to be changed—whether that be a particular situation, our attitude or actions in response to it, or both.

Feelings of stress let us know that, at some level, something's wrong and needs to be repaired. It is the thorn in our side, the pea beneath our mattress, the stick in our craw. And when recognized as such, stress can provide the motivation we need to take action.

Whether the threat is physical (a tornado headed toward our home, a stranger following us down a dark street) or strikes directly at our emotions (the breakup of a marriage); anticipated (being called into our boss's office, our spouse saying "We have got to talk") or imagined (a misinterpreted glance, the "monster" under a child's bed); whether it's financial, health-related, or falls into any one of innumerable other categories, stress is a reaction to something we perceive as a danger. Broken down to its most basic component, stress is fear.

Handled correctly, the feeling can help us correct the situation or revise our attitude toward a situation we cannot change.

When to Worry about Stress

"Sure you're tense and irritable. But don't take it out on the others." Have you heard that recently? Sometimes you can tell that stress has gotten out of line when "the others" let you know.

All of us have different stress-tolerance levels. A cross-country move might be a Level 10 stressor for Joe, but a mere blip on the scale for John. Some of that has to do with where we are in our lives: a teenager faced with establishing herself within a whole new peer group might experience far more trauma during a move than a forty-year-old who's already moved numerous times. The move might be more stressful if provoked by divorce or the loss of a job (on the other hand, the new start in life might provide welcome stress relief). A change might be less stressful if it's motivated by a long-awaited return to one's hometown.

How we react to stress in the present also depends on how we learned to handle stress in the

STREET SMARTS

Working in an occupation that suits your stress profile can radically affect your stress load. Time pressure, for instance, is a tension nightmare for some and a dream come true for others. So knowing your profile is key.

"I'm one of those adrenaline junkies," says forty-five-year-old Arthur Brice, a reporter for a daily newspaper in Atlanta. "To me, being on deadline is a great rush, so work is not a source of stress. I just love it."

past: Did we learn to bottle up our emotions and reach for a cigarette, or turn to healthful physical activity or friends and family for support?

Research has documented that gender, marital status, age, and educational background all have significant effects on stress levels. Genetics also plays a role, as does the number of stressful events occurring simultaneously. The stress impact of an event is not built into the event itself, but rather in how it affects you.

Stress has gotten out of hand when it interferes with our lives—physically or emotionally—no matter if it's a lot or a little by any scale. If you are uncomfortable, unhappy, or unhealthy, it is probably related to too much stress. Period.

Quiz 1: Is Stress Affecting Your Life?

How much of an impact is stress having on your life? Answer the following questions from the National Mental Health Association to help gauge your level of stress. The more "Yes" answers, the more cause for concern.

1. Do minor problems and disappointments upset you excessively?

2. Do the small pleasures of life fail to satisfy you?

3. Are you unable to stop thinking of your worries?

4. Do you feel inadequate or suffer from self-doubt?

5. Are you constantly tired?

6. Do you experience flashes of anger over situations which used to not bother you?

7. Have you noticed a change in sleeping or eating patterns?

8. Do you suffer from chronic pain, headache, or backache?

How the Body Registers Stress

Stress, for some of us, announces itself in tremors that would register on the Richter scale; they shake, they quiver, their fingers beat a nervous tattoo on any surface with which they come in contact. But stress appears in many a guise—some less obvious than others. One thing is certain, it's not "all in your head."

In a paper published in the *New England Journal of Medicine*, Bruce S. McEwen, Ph.D., head of the Laboratory of Neuroendocrinology at Rockefeller University in New York, identifies eight physical indicators in the body, from blood pressure to abdominal fat, that can be measured to give a tangible indication of an individual's personal stress level or "allostatic load," the term he has adopted to mean the price our bodies pay in adapting to stress.

"From the standpoint of health," says McEwen, "what is even more important than how we feel about the stressful events in our lives is how our bodies react in terms of the stress hormones they produce."

Headaches; a tight, dry throat; a clenched jaw; chest pain; shortness of breath; a pounding heart; high blood pressure; muscle aches; indigestion; increased perspiration; and insomnia are some of our bodies' reactions to stress. Others are constipation or diarrhea, lethargy or hyperactivity.

The skin and hair are other powerful barometers of stress. Acne, hives, and rashes are telltale signs; wrinkles and worry lines may also appear. Graying and loss of hair are equally relevant signs.

F.Y.I.

Number of Americans nationwide who say they are always pressed for time:

| 1982 | 25 % |
| 1998 | 32 % |

Source: Atlanta Journal-Constitution, "Southern Focus Poll"

The Stress Response

The sensation we interpret negatively as stress is actually no different from the physical feelings we experience during positive events. When we open the door to a party in our honor that we did not expect, we call it surprise. When we anticipate a first kiss, we call it exhilaration. In many ways, as far as the body is concerned, it's all one thing: An out-of-the-ordinary "attack" of emotion, which we physiologically perceive as a threat.

Whether dealing with a single experience or ongoing tension, the body responds to such threats by getting ready to attack the problem or by trying to get away from it—better known as the "fight or flight" response. A variety of hormones acts as chemical messengers to prepare us for battle or swift escape.

Corticotropin releasing factor stimulates the brain's pituitary gland to release adrenocorticotropic hormone (ACTH), which signals the adrenal gland to release more hormones, including adrenaline (epinephrine) and cortisol, which help the body to adapt or "gear up." We breathe faster, our heartbeat quickens, and our blood pressure rises. The circulatory system redirects oxygen and nutrients to organs that need more energy to function with stress, such as the brain and muscles. And energy sources such as blood sugar (glucose) and fat are released into the blood, as is fibrin, which helps the blood clot.

"The hormonal stress response is in almost every way, shape, and form a protective and adaptive response," says McEwen, author of *The Hostage Brain* with Harold M. Schmeck, Jr. "If you didn't have it you'd be dead after many ordinary situations. It's the imbalance of these stress hormone systems—if they fail to shut off when they should and work overtime—that causes problems."

How the Mind Registers Stress

Disorientation, distraction, and forgetfulness are but a few of the ways our minds tell us we're overburdened; irritability, defensiveness, and anger are a few more. Don't forget hypersensitivity, apathy, depression, and the other signs of distress that contradict the characterization of the stresser as a frantic blur of tension personified.

In other words, stress physically makes us less sensible and so more susceptible to the very emotion that may be its cause.

Sleeping and eating patterns change, interpersonal relations go awry, and we suddenly resume that teeth-grinding habit we thought we'd gotten over in childhood. Depending on the individual, job performance can begin to occur at the speed of light or can be slowed to an almost imperceptible crawl; either every little thing is worth fighting over, or nothing matters at all. Sudden and noticeable alterations in patience level, social activities, physical appearance, and personal habits may indicate an overstressed mind.

Panic Attacks

Panic attacks are to stress as atomic bombs are to bullets. Ten to 20 percent of Americans will have a

SMART MOVE

"Don't add the fear of stress to the stresses in your life," say the American Heart Association and the American Cancer Society in *Living Well, Staying Well*. Stress is a perfectly normal aspect of the human condition, experienced by us all. "Stress isn't necessarily a bad thing—it's more in how you handle it."

panic attack at some time in their lives. And there are 2.4 million others nationwide with *panic disorder,* a chronic illness where attacks are recurrent, as is the fear, palpitations, breathlessness, nausea, sweating, dizziness, tingling sensations, hot flashes or chills that come with them. These symptoms can be severe enough to prompt a trip to the emergency room and strong enough to resemble a heart attack or the descent into insanity.

Thirty percent of those 2.4 million with panic disorder develop agoraphobia, the fear of leaving home. Twenty percent attempt suicide. About 30 percent abuse alcohol; about 17 percent abuse drugs.

The difference between those with panic disorder and the rest of us seems to lie in the brain. As in other anxiety disorders, including *generalized anxiety disorder* (or GAD, which is a specific pattern of worry and fear) and *social phobias* (a dread of public embarrassment or episodes of panic attacks in specific situations, such as while waiting in line or walking the dog), panic disorder is related to marked differences in brain chemistry and activity; when it comes to the fight-or-flight response, people with panic disorder can be said to be on a hair trigger.

The good news is that the disorders are highly treatable, but they do require professional help. Behavioral or drug therapies, or a combination of the two, can provide significant relief. Contact the National Institute of Mental Health (see "Smart Sources" on page 3 to learn more).

Quiz 2: Are You Having a Panic Attack?

Typically, a first panic attack seems to come out of the blue, often at times of considerable stress. Lasting intensely for a period anywhere from seconds to minutes, and gradually fading over the course of about an hour, the symptoms are so overwhelming that victims of the attack may honestly believe they are going to die or lose their minds.

Some people have one panic attack, or an occasional attack in their lives, while others experience panic disorder, a condition that calls for the attention of a health-care professional. During any one attack, some or all of the following symptoms occur. If you can identify with one or more of these, and have been experiencing them to an extent that is seriously affecting your life, seek professional help.

• A sense of terror or that something unimaginably horrible is about to happen and you're powerless to do anything about it

• Difficulty breathing

• Tingling or numbness in the hands

• Flushes or chills

• Sense of unreality

• Fear of losing control, going "crazy," or doing something embarrassing

• Fear of dying

• Heart palpitations

• Dizziness

Tips

• **Assess the situation and remind yourself that you are not in real danger.** Although your feelings and symptoms are frightening, they are not life threatening. They are just an exaggerated version of your body's normal reaction to stress.

• **Do not fight your feelings or try to wish them away.** The more you are willing to face and accept them, the less intense they will become in a relatively short period of time.

• **Stay in the present and avoid the "what if" syndrome:** constantly wondering what might happen in the future, often asking yourself, "What if . . . ?" The answers to such questions should be, "So what!"

• **Rate your fear level from zero to ten.** Notice the fluctuations. It won't remain at very high levels for more than a few seconds at a time.

• **Distract yourself.** For example, count the number of blue things that are in the room, practice the multiplication tables, or do a simple exercise.

• **Remember that ultimately everything will be all right.** By not adding frightening thoughts to your fear, you will help it fade away.

Stress-Related Illness

Stress can make you sick.

When sustained to the point that it becomes chronic, or its assaults are at levels beyond the body's capability to cope with in a healthy way, the stress response meant to help us can do harm.

There is evidence of its role in gastrointestinal, dermatological, respiratory, neurologic, and emotional ills, as well as proof of its impact on a wide range of infections and disorders linked to immune system disturbances—from the common cold to herpes and arthritis. The risk of bacterial infections such as tuberculosis increases during highly stressful times, as does the susceptibility to upper respiratory viral infections. Stress may also worsen symptoms of asthma and gastrointestinal problems such as ulcer or irritable bowel syndrome.

High stress levels are associated with increases in heart disease risk factors such as high blood pressure and high cholesterol levels. If you're a "hot reactor," according to the *Mayo Clinic Health Letter,* acute stress can present big trouble: "As a response to daily stress, hot reactors exhibit extreme increases in heart rate and blood pressure. According to the theory, these surges may gradually result in injury to your coronary arteries and heart. When stress persists, increased blood clotting as a result of the stress response can put you at risk for a heart attack or stroke."

Bruce McEwen's studies at Rockefeller University have found that a higher allostatic load can lead to suppression of the body's immune system, as well as to bone loss, muscular weakening, atherosclerosis, and increased insulin levels. These increased insulin levels can, in turn, increase the amount of fat that is deposited in the body, especially around the abdomen. This results in the "apple" body shape that has been associated with an increased risk of heart disease.

Many other studies are exploring the role of

Signs of Stress

- Change in appetite
- Change in sleeping patterns
- Skin outbreaks
- Shortened temper
- Change in sexual appetite
- Forgetfulness or absentmindedness
- Increase in smoking or drinking of alcohol
- Change in weight
- Difficulty breathing
- Recurring colds, illnesses, or chronic infections
- Trembling
- Heart palpitations
- Excessive perspiration

F.Y.I.

Percent of visits to physicians that are stress-related:

75 to 90 percent

Amount spent annually by businesses on job stress–related health-care costs:

$150 million

Source: National Mental Health Association

the mind in influencing the risks of cancer. Much research links stress to the suppression of immune system function, and a strong immune system is believed to be crucial to preventing the disease.

A study published in the *Journal of Advancement in Medicine* found that "replaying" for a five-minute period an event that made subjects angry could suppress levels of an immune-system antibody for six hours.

Another study published in the American Psychological Association's *Journal of Personality and Social Psychology* examined the effect of optimism in the context of a stressor—in this case, the first year of law school—on mood and immune changes in a healthy population. While there were no immune differences between optimists and pessimists before beginning law school, students who began the semester optimistic were found to have higher levels of function for key immune cells; these cells are linked with immunity against viral infection and some cancers. The study attributed changes in the immune system to two psychological characteristics of optimists: they experience events as less stressful, and they show less negative mood.

While researchers are continuing to explore the impact of emotions and stress on hormones and the immune system and the links of stressors to cancer and cardiac, respiratory, and other diseases, there is no question that stress can harm us via the self-destructive behaviors it can provoke. Smoking, drinking, substance abuse, bad dietary habits, and lack of exercise are all proven, direct links to ill health.

The Age of Anxiety

A revised version of a 1965 stressful-event checklist, used to measure the connection between stress and illness, rates seventy-four life-change events (having a child, losing a job, relocation, and so on) by the stress they might generate. Rated by volunteers who were demographically similar to those who participated in the initial study, the impact of these life changes was found to be on average 45 percent more stressful today than they were thirty years ago.

"Life stress, as estimated by recent life change magnitude estimations, appears to have increased markedly across the past thirty years," report researchers Mark A. Miller and Richard H. Rahe in the *Journal of Psychosomatic Research.* The influences of these life events, they note, "seem to be increasing at a steady rate." (See the "Life Changes Questionnaire" in chapter 2.)

For the one or two people who were uncertain, in other words, now there's official scientific proof: even with all our modern psycho-savvy and self-help awareness, today's society feels the influence of stressors more strongly than ever before.

Why? The disappearance of the hometown community, prompted in no small part by job-relocation demands, has stripped us of the familiar, supportive structure on which we once could rely. Families are now spread far and wide; relationships are scattered to the winds.

Add to that a changing economic

Anxiety Survey

An ongoing, interactive Internet survey begun in 1997 on the topic of stress and honesty recorded almost two thousand responses when we last investigated. Among its questions: "How often do you experience severe anxiety in your life, to the point that it hinders your ability to function?"

26.0 %	Never
19.8 %	Every few years
24.1 %	A few times a year
10.9 %	Once a month
16.0 %	Once a week or more
3.2 %	*No response*

Source: Survey.net

climate that has today's generation feeling less well-off than their parents in poll after poll; the harried two-income households that have become the norm; urban sprawl that crams us next to neighbors whose names we don't even know; and chemicals in our air and water whose effects we can only guess. Even the national parks that once provided escape are now so overcrowded that access to them involves dealing with long lines and traffic snarls.

We are tired, we are lonely, we are out of shape. And we are lacking the very stress defenses we need more than ever before.

Cyberstress

The burgeoning array of stressors among which we lived a decade ago prompted *Time* magazine to run a cover story referring to stress as the "epidemic of the eighties." Since then, the disease can only be said to have metastasized. As we approach the twenty-first century, we can safely say to *Time,* "You ain't seen nothing yet."

Since the eighties, "technostress," "information overload," or what we call "cyberstress" has multiplied exponentially at rates that only a computer could . . . compute.

Without even calculating the performance anxiety caused by technology that seems to update itself by the minute, and the financial demands such updates present, the tidal wave of information with which we are now confronted at home and on the job is drowning us in more data than we can—or should have to—possibly endure.

"As we have accrued more and more of it, information has emerged not only as a currency but also as a pollutant," writes David Shenk in *Data Smog: Surviving the Information Glut.*

Shenk gives us the numbers: while in 1971 the average American was targeted with at least 560 daily advertising messages, twenty years later that number had risen to 3,000. In the 1980s, the volume of delivery of third-class mail—junk mail— grew thirteen times as fast as the population.

Of "the noxious muck and druck of the information age," Shenk says, "data smog gets in the way, and it crowds out quiet moments and obstructs much-needed contemplation. It spoils conversation, literature, and even entertainment. It thwarts skepticism, rendering us less sophisticated as consumers and citizens. It stresses us out."

Shenk's Fourth Law of Data Smog: "What they sell is not information technology, but information anxiety."

William Gibson would not be surprised. The man who coined the word *cyberspace* in his sci-fi novel *Neuromancer* foresaw a dark future of information overload disease called nerve attenuation syndrome, otherwise known as the "black shakes."

To avoid the "black shakes" and other dangers of stress overload, you first need to learn how to identify your personal stressors. Chapter 2 will show you the way.

THE BOTTOM LINE

Stress is an unavoidable part of life, but it doesn't have to be a disabling one. The more we know about how it affects us, and why, the less opportunity it has to take hold of us, and the more opportunity we have to either circumvent it altogether or to put it to work on our own behalf. We can change our situation, change the way we view it, and even change both.

CHAPTER 2

The Leading Causes of Stress

THE KEYS

• Knowing the types of stress to which we're susceptible can help us lessen—or avert—their effects.

• At the heart of all anxiety lies a fear of being out of control and being powerless to impact one or more aspects of our own lives.

• Individual temperament is the key to identifying vulnerability to stress.

• To everything there is a season, and stress is no exception.

• Environment plays an important role as the backdrop to stress susceptibility levels.

Whoever and wherever you are, man or woman, on the job or at home, stress will find a way of finding you. But just as not all of us are alike in terms of our response to it, not all types of stress are alike in terms of their relevance to our lives. Finding our Achilles' heel—the type of stresses to which we're most susceptible—can help us avert or deal with what stresses us most.

Powerlessness

"I've lost all control!" "I'm out of control!" "Get a hold of yourself!" "Get a grip!"

If those phrases sound all too familiar—either because you find the first two coming from your mouth or often hear the others coming in your direction—it's no wonder you're stressed. Research has time and again found that those with a sense of control over their lives are more resistant to stress's negative effects.

Feelings of powerlessness are frustrating, that is, stressful. One of the theories that would explain why women and minorities experience greater stress levels is their traditionally low level on the power totem pole. "Control is a major ingredient in stress," says Simone Ravicz, Ph.D., M.B.A., author of *High on Stress: A Woman's Guide to Optimizing the Stress in Her Life.* "When you perceive that you have control it can really transform what you see as negative and threatening to positive and challenging."

Workers whose jobs allow them to make decisions are less likely to feel the frustrations—and the stress—felt by those who are at the mercy of supervisors' directives, or those who have to do battle constantly with uncooperative coworkers or underlings.

"Having a job that places a high demand on producing a product or a service with very little decision-making power has also been found to further fuel hostility, depression, and social isolation," said Redford B. Williams, M.D., director of the Behavioral Medicine Research Center at Duke University Medical Center and coauthor of *Anger Kills,* who studied the effects of such factors on the mortality rates of 1,368 patients with coronary disease.

But while in many ways all stress can be traced back to issues of control, the areas where powerlessness is experienced differ from person to person and change at varying times and places in each one of our lives.

Time Pressure

The image of the person running breathlessly to catch a plane, scurrying to prepare for a business meeting, or working frantically to meet a deadline is the picture of anxiety. Too much to do in too little time is the most common complaint in stress-management seminars.

Some of this can be blamed on our have-it-all approach to life. Career, family, friends, community activism, a fashionable wardrobe, the right hairstyle, trips and vacations at the best resorts—all bear equal weight on lengthy must-have lists.

"One of the main reasons Americans are so stressed is that we pack so much into our lives, yet we don't prioritize anything," says Catherine Solheim, associate professor with the Department of

Family and Child Development, in the *Auburn University News.* "'Everything must be done now and everything is important' is our mentality."

And we're indoctrinated early.

"Parents and families need downtime, time to be families and time to let kids be kids," says Solheim, who teaches stress management in her family- and child-development classes. "We run home from a busy day at work, pick up the kids, eat fast food, and then act as chauffeur to our kids, taking them to a variety of after-school activities. We do not have time in our lives to slow down, and we've packed our kids' free time with activities so they can't slow down either.

Without a realistic schedule, we don't have control of our time.

"Some people believe they are good time managers but probably are not," says Mayo Clinic psychologist Donald E. Williams, Ph.D., in the online newsletter Health O@sis. "They take few breaks and may have many 'minor' health complaints. Others might say, 'I'm very busy, I get a lot done, but I'm stressed out at the end of the day.' These are the people who are probably not managing time well in terms of stress."

Money Matters

We've heard it said that "time is money." In terms of stress-producing potential, money is right up there with time; the two are vying for first place. Financial deficits can wrest control from us in almost every facet of life, from housing to health care to, yes, the time we have available to do the things we want. (Who among us has not cried out for a maid, a cook, or perhaps a personal shopper during the holiday crunch?)

"Debt is certainly a stressor and it certainly has increased," says Gerri Detweiler, education advisor with Debt Counselors of America and author of *Invest in Yourself: Six Secrets to a Rich Life.*

"Despite an expanding economy, Americans are increasingly experiencing financial difficulties," Detweiler adds. Credit card debt more than doubled between 1990 and 1996, and stood at $455 billion as the fourth quarter of 1997 got under way.

While debt burdens have increased, savings rates have dropped, and the number of families reporting that they spent less than their income declined. One report put the 1997 year-end savings rate at a fifty-eight-year low. And around one-third of us are continually worried about our ability to pay our bills.

"There are substantial costs to employers caused by the stresses associated with the poor personal financial behaviors of employees," says E. Thomas Garman, Ed.D., professor of consumer affairs and family financial management at Virginia Polytechnic Institute and State University. "This is the most glossed-over and ignored worker issue today."

Of course, the effect is not confined to the office. Financial problems are usually complex, and straightforward, rational solutions do little to address emotional or psychological needs. Again, in many cases, the problem can be traced to a lack of control. In a research project on women and finance, Detweiler found "one of the big issues that emerged was a feeling that they were not in control."

F.Y.I.

Number of Americans who declared bankruptcy in 1987:

495,553

Number of Americans who declared bankruptcy in 1997:

More than 1,350,188

Source: American Bankruptcy Institute

SMART SOURCES

Debt Counselors of
   America
P.O. Box 8587
Gaithersburg, MD
   20898
800-680-3328
www.dca.org

Everything you've ever
wanted to know about
getting out of debt—
and much more than
you would ever have
thought to ask—is
available with a toll-
free phone call or a
visit to this nonprofit
organization's richly
stocked Web site.
Choose from a library
of helpful information,
online chats with
experts, and scam
alerts.

Keeping Up with the Joneses

Keeping up can be a very dangerous thing.

Comparisons to the people around you—whether they are the Joneses next door, your older brother Steve, or Rhea in the office just down the hall—are shortcuts to disappointment. People who share your world simply are not the same as you and have different resources, or resources allocated differently than yours. The neighbor with the new car, the new big-screen TV, and the new high-priced gardener might have just won the lottery, or lost a wealthy relative. The guy who gets so much done at the office might be the sort whom others would encourage to "get a life," while you have a spouse, two kids, three dogs, Little League practice, a weekly card game, and a passion for bird-watching that demand quite a bit of your energy, attention, and time.

Those who model their lives on those of supermodels might be on track if they're looking for tips on makeup techniques, fashion, or exercise routines but not if they're expecting to reach superhigh standards that might not exist even for the models themselves. Comparing yourself to someone whose body is her profession and who spends hours a day in the gym and salon with professional stylists and trainers is dooming yourself to failure—and all the stress that comes with knocking your head against a wall. Remember, too, that you might be comparing yourself to fantasy: the wonders of computer photo-imaging can make a flawed complexion look perfect and eliminate cellulite without exercise or scalpel.

The Superhero Complex

The pursuit of impossibility takes another form in the Superhero Complex: the conviction that if you just try hard enough or spend enough you will be faster than a speeding bullet, more powerful than a locomotive, and able to leap tall buildings in a single bound. A close relative of perfectionism, this self-destructive pursuit of attaining a nonhuman ideal is a losing battle. Instead of accomplishing all those feats we set out to, we may well end up accomplishing none. Instead of inviting friends over for dinner, we obsess about the food, the wine, the drink, the silver, the house, and our wardrobe until we've convinced ourselves there's no way we're up to the task. Instead of handing in the inventory assessment our boss asked for on Monday, we retype and retype it, only to find the week (and our deadline) long gone.

We cannot do everything or be everything, simply because we cannot do or be *anything* that does not have some flaw. Striving for perfection in aspects of life is fine, as long as we don't really expect to get there.

Chemical Causes

Stress is not all in the mind—neither in terms of its effect on the body *nor* in terms of the effect that the body can have on susceptibility to stress.

Nicotine, caffeine, alcohol, marijuana, drugs and medications, and other substances that we put

Stress-Building Beliefs

The Center for Anxiety and Stress Treatment in La Jolla, California, suggests the following questions for employees to get in touch with their stress-building beliefs. The questions apply to other aspects of life as well. The more "yes" answers, the more of a stress builder you are—and that's not something you want to be.

Perfectionism

Do you feel a constant pressure to achieve?

Do you criticize yourself when you're not perfect?

Do you feel you haven't done enough no matter how hard you try?

Do you give up pleasure in order to be the best in everything you do?

Control

Do you have to be perfectly in control at all times?

Do you worry about how you appear to others when you are nervous?

Do you feel that any lack of control is a sign of weakness or failure?

Are you uncomfortable delegating projects to others?

People Pleasing

Does your self-esteem depend on everyone else's opinion of you?

Do you sometimes avoid assignments because you're afraid of disappointing your boss?

Are you better at caring for others than caring for yourself?

Do you keep most negative feelings inside to avoid displeasing others?

Competence

Do you feel you can never do as good a job as other people?

Do you feel your judgment is poor?

Do you feel you lack common sense?

Do you feel like an impostor when told your work is good?

Source: Overcoming Panic, Anxiety and Phobias, Shirley Babior, L.C.S.W.; and Carol Goldman, L.I.C.S.W.; and the Center for Anxiety and Stress Treatment. www.stressrelease.com.

into the body—or withdraw from—can make us more susceptible to stress or even trigger the stress response.

Cigarettes

If the thought of the numerous health risks associated with smoking aren't stressful enough to keep you from lighting up, here are a few more reasons to quit. Not only do the debilitating effects of the habit physically increase vulnerability to stress but the nicotine in cigarettes is a *sympathomimetic,* a substance that stimulates the body into the stress response. The fleeting feeling of calm so many smokers associate with their cigarette breaks is not due to any true sedative effect of the nicotine; it's merely a temporary "fix" in a nicotine addiction that is causing the irritability and anxiety in the first place.

Alcohol

Alcohol is another substance that may temporarily seem to relax you but, with overuse, will add more stress as it taxes the body's detoxification system, throws off blood-sugar balance, and reduces levels of vitamins and minerals that are important in combating stress's negative effects.

Drugs

Even seemingly harmless over-the-counter cold, allergy, and sinus medications can bring on many of the symptoms of stress. Sympathomimetics such as epinephrine, norephinephrine, ephedrine, and others are often common ingredients. Also, medications prescribed for asthmatics, diabetics, or patients with thyroid conditions can cause stress responses, as can withdrawal from a wide range of antidepressants; even the monosodium glutamate (MSG) in Chinese dinners can prompt symptoms of anxiety.

Diet

When your body is experiencing some type of stress, experts believe that nutritional requirements change, and the body demands more B-complex vitamins, protein, and calcium, among other vitamins and minerals. The opposite also applies: changing your diet can have a direct effect on stress.

"What you eat can increase your negative stress level both directly and indirectly," writes Simone Ravicz in *High on Stress*. "Certain foods create too much wear and tear on our bodies by propelling it into a negative stress response or by overusing its detoxification system."

The two main culprits: sugar and caffeine. "If you feel perpetually wound up, stressed out, jittery, restless, unable to relax or sleep, and have a racing heart and don't suffer from a medical condition causing such symptoms," says Ravicz, "you are probably using a great deal."

Caffeine—not just in your morning coffee, but in tea, colas, chocolate, and other favorites—revs up the nervous, cardiac, and respiratory systems; contributes to the depletion of vitamins and minerals; and causes the release of adrenaline. Like other

The Circle of Stress and Health

In chapter 1 we explored the connection between stress and the body, including the damage that an ongoing stress response can wreak. A variety of ailments, from hypertension and heart attack to headaches, stomach trouble, and asthma can flare up and the immune system can be compromised, making us susceptible to a range of infectious diseases. Stress may aggravate an existing health problem or trigger an illness if we're at risk.

But there's a flip side to that. When we're not in good health, we're also more susceptible to stress. If our body is worn down from improper nutrition, lack of sleep, or illness, our stress-fighting skills suffer as well. The chihuahua puppy that you find adorable ordinarily is transformed into a four-legged anxiety machine when you have a toothache. The hectic schedule you're used to is impossible after a sleepless night. Deficiencies in vitamins and minerals leave your body less able to cope.

Other times, symptoms of stress can be mistaken for disease, which is stressful in itself. A palpating heart, a turning stomach, rashes, or tremors can bring out the hypochondriac in us all. Even some physicians overlook the stress component.

"Some people are well aware that their demands are too high and therefore their stress is high," writes clinical psychologist Donald Williams, a consultant in Behavioral Medicine at the Mayo Clinic in Rochester, Minnesota. "But others . . . tend to respond to stress with bodily complaints. . . . They may get headaches. They may get chest pains. They go to their doctor, who may or may not recognize it as stress related. The doctor may treat the symptoms, which is important, but treatment of symptoms may not get at the root cause.

"You don't want to write something off as stress when it may be a medical problem," Williams elaborates. "On the other hand, if a medical problem is identified, it doesn't necessarily rule stress out."

sympathomimetics, it not only stimulates the stress response but also makes the nervous system more reactive, and so increases susceptibility to stress.

Refined sugar dramatically activates the sympathetic nervous system and increases the level of blood sugar, which the body interprets as a sign that we must be in a fight-or-flight situation.

By reducing the artificially stimulated stress responses in your life, you can help yourself to respond in a more controlled way to real stressors when they do occur.

Living in Chaos

Ask the stress-savvy for a definition of disorganization and the answer will come hard and fast: A physical manifestation of lack of control. Think of something you want and know you have—somewhere. Then imagine how you feel when you can't find it anywhere you look. Searching, digging, excavating, praying. You're powerless over your environment, and that's stressful.

Disorganization can find you forgetting to record that lunch-date appointment and have you frantically trying to hunt down directions to the restaurant thirty minutes before you're due to sit down at the table . . . which, you suddenly learn, is forty-five minutes away. (And, of course, you can't find the map and directions to get there.)

You don't necessarily have to be neat to be organized. We've all known the feeling of being baffled by a newly straightened closet or drawer. The key is in having a system—of any kind—that you understand.

Life Changes

Change—for better *or* for worse—can be stressful. Whether you just got a great new job or were fired from the position you held for years, or whether you just brought a new child into your home or recently lost a loved one to illness, change puts big demands on your ability to cope.

"Social readjustment scales measure the intensity and length of time necessary to accommodate to a life event," explain researchers Mark A. Miller and Richard H. Rahe, who devised a checklist to measure potential stress load, "regardless of the desirability of this event."

Miller and Rahe's questionnaire assigns stress points, or Life Change Units (LCUs), based on the amount of change resulting from a wide range of life events. Read the following list of events and record the points if it applies to you. Total your score at the end.

Life Changes Questionnaire

Health

An injury or illness that:
    kept you in bed a week or more,
        or sent you to the hospital 74
    was less serious than that 44
Major dental work 26
Major change in eating habits 27
Major change in sleeping habits 26
Major change in your usual type
    or amount of recreation 28

STREET SMARTS

In Tulsa, Oklahoma, the Jackson family has turned their stress-coping into a science. "I love to cook, but having the family over for a big special dinner entirely stresses me out," says Arlene, a twenty-nine-year-old dental assistant. "For my husband, whose only worries involve cars and the stock market, entertaining is a breeze. Whenever we have relatives over, he cooks, I clean up afterward, and nobody gets indigestion."

Work

Home and Family

Child leaving home:

    to attend college 41

    due to marriage 41

    for other reasons 45

Change in arguments with spouse 50

In-law problems 38

Change in the marital status of your parents:

    divorce 59

    remarriage 50

Separation from spouse:

    due to work 53

    due to marital problems 76

Divorce 96

Birth of grandchild 43

Death of spouse 119

Death of other family member:

    child 123

    brother or sister 102

    parent 100

Personal and Social

Change in personal habits 26

Beginning or ending school or college 38

Change of school or college 35

Change in political beliefs 24

Change in religious beliefs 29

Change in social activities 27

Vacation trip 24

New close personal relationship 37

Engagement to marry 45

Girlfriend or boyfriend problems 39

Sexual difficulties 44

"Falling out" of a close personal

    relationship 47

An accident 48

Minor violation of the law 20

Being held in jail 75

Death of a close friend 70

Major decision about your
   immediate future 51
Major personal achievement 36

Financial

Major change in finances:
   increased income 38
   decreased income 60
   investment or credit difficulties 56
Loss or damage of personal property 43
Moderate purchase 20
Major purchase 37
Foreclosure on a mortgage or loan 58

Tally the points for those you experienced in *either* the past six months or the past year. A six-month total equal to or greater than 300 points or a one-year total equal to or greater than 500 points are considered indicative of high recent life stress.

Whom It's Most Likely to Strike

Gender, age, and marital status are just a few of the many variables that influence our reaction to different kinds of stress.

In a culture such as ours, which places great emphasis on female physical appearance, women tend to be more concerned about such issues as weight control and wrinkled skin. In their role as caretakers, women may be more greatly affected by what's going on in the lives of others around them than their male counterparts might be. Men, on the other hand, are more often stressed by "he man" issues, such as their standing in the office pecking order, their ability to financially support their families, and their maintenance of the image that they can handle anything and everything—including stress—on their own. This may account for the finding in one study that women tend to view life changes as more stressful than men do but they also tend to act more quickly and effectively to alleviate their distress.

"It appears that women both assess and react to life stress events at higher levels than men," reported researchers Miller and Rahe in the *Journal of Psychosomatic Research* after finding women rated all but one of eighty-seven life-change events as more stressful than did men. Rather than interpreting the phenomenon as a sign that women are "overreactors," the researchers found it more likely that men "underreact," pointing to studies that revealed a tendency for men to repress and deny very severe symptoms of illness. Men almost defensively repress and deny the impact of their stressors as well. (More on gender differences in chapter 6.)

As we journey through life, different issues concern us, and their impact varies. For children, it might be the "monster" under the bed, fear of the dark, or the unknown. For teens, it is often peer approval and academic pressure. A few years later, we're victims of the "get married–have kids" push. Adults often list family, finances, and work at the top of their stress list. Later on in life, health concerns and social isolation take center stage. Both middle-aged adults and youth tend to view change as more stressful than do their elders. Apparently, the more experience you have in life, the easier it is to take things in stride.

People who are married, and others with a healthy support system to which they can turn dur-

SMART MOVE

"People say other people have lives that are worse than theirs or contain more stressors," says Donald E. Williams, Ph.D., of the Mayo Clinic in Rochester, Minnesota. "While that may be true, it's irrelevant to a given individual's health. What is stressful to you is stressful to you and healthwise that's all that matters."

ing times of hardship, have been found to fare better when stressed. Even with the additional demands that family and friends present, the knowledge just that they are there to turn to can make things easier to take in stride.

"Laboratory research shows cardiovascular responses to acute mental stressors can be reduced when social support is provided to the experimental subjects," concluded Duke University's Redford Williams in his coronary-patient study. Fifty percent of the patients who reported feeling very isolated, were not married, and had no one in whom they could confide died within five years, compared to 17 percent of those with either a spouse or confidant.

"These higher death rates among socially isolated heart patients could not be explained by any differences in the severity of the underlying heart disease," said Williams. "People need to realize that they need each other to stay healthy."

When It's Most Likely to Strike

To everything there is a season, and stress is by no means an exception.

Holidays—and all the expectations associated with them—are particular times to beware. From the anticipated revelry of New Year's Eve to the romance of Valentine's Day; from Fourth of July barbecues to Christmas, Hanukkah, or Kwanza and the gift-giving, card-sending, entertaining blur they've become, celebratory pressure can take its toll.

In addition to all the routine goings-on of life,

holidays add entertaining and visiting, decorating and gifts, cooking, guests who stay over, and financial strain. Add to this the pressure to be relaxed and happy everywhere you turn, and special-event stress can be especially troublesome.

Beyond presenting the challenges of additional responsibilities and expectations, holidays present situations that differ from our usual day-to-day life. When we're used to something and know what to expect from it—be it the behavior of the teenagers down the street or our boss's Monday morning bad mood—we enjoy a comfortable sense of control.

Even familiar discomfort can be preferable to strange, new pleasures, as is evident from the many who will opt for known evils over the potential for joy. We're not known as "creatures of habit" without reason.

Where It's Most Likely to Strike

Environment has a lot to do with stress level. Just as basking in pastel tones can be calming, being surrounded by nerve-shattering hues can overly stimulate our overwrought brains. Add noise, a few neighbors too close for comfort, and all you'll need is a straw to break your back. Overstimulation. Overpopulation. We're all familiar with those studies of rats going cannibalistic in such a setting, and we don't need to have whiskers and tails to share that effect.

The World Health Organization (WHO) warns of the impact of global population growth and the urbanization of our planet. From 1950 to 1985,

WHAT MATTERS, WHAT DOESN'T

What Matters
• Identifying the things that are most stressful to *you*.

• Lessening the effects of or eradicating the negative stressors in your life.

• Developing a healthy, realistic attitude toward stress.

• Learning to transform stress into a useful source of energy.

What Doesn't
• Attacking or fleeing all stressors at once.

• Enduring stress solely because it will "make you a better person."

• Trying to avoid *all* stress.

F.Y.I.

The population of our planet has reached 5.7 billion people, and it is estimated that 90 million people will be added each year through the end of the century.

Fact: 30 to 50 percent of workers in industrialized countries complain of psychological stress and overload.

Source: World Health Organization

the number of cities in the industrialized world with a population greater than one million more than doubled; such cities quintupled in Asia, Africa, Latin America, and the Pacific Rim.

Heavy traffic, pollution, public transportation problems, high levels of noise, and overcrowded living conditions accompany such urbanization, which is in turn "accompanied by increases in rates of alcohol and illicit drug abuse, violence and aggression, as well as in the number of suicides," WHO reports. "All of these could not but tell upon the mental health of nations."

Perceptions matter, too. The *Atlanta Journal-Constitution* "Southern Focus Poll" found rural Southerners "much more likely" than their suburban or city counterparts to say they always felt rushed, a phenomenon that Jagdish Sheth, an Emory University futurist, blamed on the intrusion of technology—and its quickening pace—into less populous areas.

"The rural lifestyle is changing, and it's changing rapidly," Sheth told the *Journal-Constitution* in response to the survey. "Since the poll is based on the perception that people have of their life, someone who is used to being rushed [such as a city dweller] doesn't see any change. But someone who is used to a tranquil life all of a sudden feels rushed a lot more."

Here are just a few tips to help you cope in your own environment. See if you can come up with others.

Tips

• **Color your world pleasant.** When North Carolina Sheriff Gerald K. Hege had county jail cells painted pink with blue teddy bears, it wasn't because he thought it would be flattering to the prisoners' or please the younger felons. His goal: To keep inmates calm. It worked. Warm, soothing shades are easier on the mind and on the eyes.

• **Your home is your castle.** Just because you don't have a moat around it doesn't mean you have to let the unpleasant sounds, sights, or smells of the outside world intrude. Invest in good insulation and window treatments.

• **Respect yourself, and your own tastes and preferences.** An environment that's paradise for one may be Hades to another. Don't decorate or surround yourself with stylish items that aren't comforting. Don't force yourself into country living if the bright lights of the big city appeal to you.

• **Give yourself room to breathe.** It doesn't have to be the wide open spaces of the Western prairie, but wherever you are—at work or at home—allocate a small area that's just yours, and fill it with what makes you smile: a piece of your child's artwork, a photograph, some potpourri.

To learn more about how our environment can affect stress level, read on. The next chapter details the many locations and arenas where we most often come face-to-face with stress: at home, at work, and on the road.

THE BOTTOM LINE

Stress is what you feel when the demands on your life exceed your ability to meet them. You feel you're out of control. Overwhelmed. Overcome. The spectrum of stressors is a broad one, from time pressure to environmentally induced wear-and-tear. And although finances might be the number one stressor in America according to some surveys, organization might be number one for you. For all of us, stress is unavoidable. But by knowing the types of stress to which we're most susceptible, we can target our energies where they count.

Where Stress Will Find You

THE KEYS

• The American Dream version of family life is often far from the reality we face daily in our own homes; realigning our expectations can help.

• Living alone doesn't have to mean being alone; a family of friends can help us do more than "get by."

• As we labor longer and harder every day, cutting stress levels needs to be Job Number One.

• The escape from working in the corporate world to working at home replaces organizational stressors with on-your-own concerns.

• Defensive driving takes on a whole new meaning as we attempt to put the brakes to the Road Rage phenomenon.

Even as the physical and emotional responses to stressors vary from person to person, different types of anxiety can be associated with particular aspects of life familiar to us all. The Smart Guide's later chapters present stress-relieving strategies and solutions that can be applied to every variety of stress; here we address why—and how—anxiety plagues us day to day.

At Home

The Nest. Our Castle. Where the heart is. Whatever you call it, home is the place to which we look for the three R's of stress relief: relaxation, replenishment, and renewal. The reality is that home itself can be the setting for a wide variety of stressors, from interpersonal squabbles to the time and energy it takes to maintain the homestead.

All in the Family

Spouses, children, parents, grandparents, and in-laws. Throw in a few crazy aunts, uncles, and cousins and you have the family most of us know all too well. And it's not the one from the television series *Father Knows Best*. Even in the sweetest of homes, the phrase "nuclear family" can at times seem almost synonymous with "nuclear war." But targeting the most prevalent stressors can be a slippery task.

"The problem is that there's nothing generic you can say about any kind of stress," says Paul J. Rosch, M.D., president of the American Institute of Stress (AIS), and professor of medicine and psychiatry at New York Medical College. "If you talk about families you have to distinguish small families living in the city from close-knit families living in rural areas from disadvantaged and minority groups, and so on.

"The only general thing you can say is that family stress has increased dramatically over the past few decades because of increasing disruption of close social relationships, and that's often due to the fact that there are more and more single parents, working parents who don't have time for their kids, influences from television, and different role models than we had fifty years ago. All these are new and pressing problems. The most pressing is nobody has enough time."

According to the Families and Work Institutes National Study of the Changing Workforce, a five-year survey of nearly three thousand employees that examined the interconnection between work and home, nearly 30 percent of employees feel they "often" or "very often" don't have enough time for their family or important others in their lives because of their job. Another 61 percent "sometimes" feel that way.

And our jobs aren't the only time grabbers.

"We're trying to balance time that we spend with our spouse, our children, our immediate family such as aunts, uncles, and cousins, and, of course, friends," says psychotherapist Melinda A. Shoemaker, Ph.D., L.M.H.C., P.A., director of Associates in Psychological Care in Boca Raton, Florida. She places lack of time management at the head of the family-anxiety list. "People don't know how to prioritize their time, and this creates tremendous amounts of stress."

Not only do we often need help establishing our

SMART MOVE

What is one of the biggest mistakes we make in trying to reduce or cure stress? "Not recognizing that there are stresses you can do something about and those that you can't do something about," says American Institute of Stress president Paul J. Rosch, M.D., editor of *Stress Medicine.* "[Otherwise, you're] Don Quixote, tilting at windmills rather than using your time and effort where they can be most effective."

individual priorities, but as members of a family, those priorities need to be harmonious with those of the people with whom we live. Harmonious—not identical. Your spouse's weekend priority might be to visit family while yours might be to catch up on some precious time alone. Acknowledging one another's desires and negotiating a plan (say, a Saturday "date night," and Sunday brunch at the in-laws) is the only way to avoid the stress such conflicts inevitably cause. Allocating the time to negotiate is important. The quandary: You need to make time to plan time, and when time is the issue, that is much easier said than done.

Increased financial pressures are another concern. In addition to the disheartening economic trends we talked about in chapter 2, we're blessed with longer lives, which means we also have to care for those lives for a longer period of time. And while few of us would discount the joy of having our parents with us for many more years, the economic and emotional pressures of caring for an elderly parent can be considerable.

Add to that the fact that more children are living at home longer, resulting in a "sandwich generation" of baby boomers who find their caretaking demands coming from both sides. And more families are headed by Mom or Dad alone.

As women have left the home for the workforce over the past twenty years, families have also had to cope with child-care issues and a reshuffling of family roles for every member of the household. That isn't necessarily a bad thing. Women, for instance, have traditionally tended to take on the more repetitive and routine household chores, whereas men are involved in non-repetitive tasks. Asks psychotherapist Shoemaker, "So who do you think gets burned out quicker?"

Establishing a set of new and appropriate roles and boundaries is essential to reducing conflict and stress.

Neither are children exempt from stressors. Expectations of parents and teachers, peer pressure, violence in the schools, and other anxiety-raisers often go unnoticed by older siblings and parents focusing on their own numerous grown-up concerns.

F.Y.I.

Percentage of single-parent families:

1970	11 %
1997	28 %

Number of adult children living at home:

1970	15 million
1997	22 million

Source: U.S. Census Bureau

Home Alone

The absence of relationships—with family, with a spouse, with friends, neighbors, or coworkers—leaves us on our own, without a shoulder to cry on when we need one, without the "attaboys" we crave when we have a triumph to announce, and without the sheer joy of sharing life's pleasurable experiences with another human being.

Despite all the adulation our society pays the single life and its kick-up-your-heels image, there's great pressure on both men and women to settle down. (And if you are single and aren't kicking up those heels, there's pressure to do that, as well.)

There is statistical proof that those who are true "loners" (and it is important to differentiate them from individuals who live alone but interact with others outside the home) will live shortened lives. In part, yes, we can attribute this to not having someone around when we've fallen and can't get up, but the emotional factors have an undeniable effect. Lack of human companionship, chronic loneliness, social isolation, and the sudden loss of a loved one are among the leading contributors to premature death in North America. Across boundaries of age, gender, and race, death rates for the single, those who are widowed, and the divorced—or unhappily married—range from two to ten times higher than for "happily" married individuals. Alternatively, social interaction has been documented to reduce stress hormone levels and their harms.

When we're in social relationships, or attempt-

Blended Families

In more and more homes, divorce, remarriage, and a staggering array of alternative domestic arrangements have created a cacophony of stepmothers, ex-husbands, half-siblings, and significant others. In the words of family therapists John and Emily Visher, it's no longer a family tree, it's a "family forest."

The stresses implicit in the "blending" of families range from step-sibling rivalry to mom-and-pop one-upmanship to the anxieties caused by the commingling of religions, traditions, and backgrounds. Both children and parents can be taxed. "The majority of families today are blended or reconstituted families," says psychotherapist Melinda A. Shoemaker, Ph.D., L.M.H.C.. P.A. "This produces a tremendous amount of stress for children in particular."

"In the beginning especially, there are a lot of new complications and stresses because the family is trying to establish and redefine its relationships," says marriage and family therapist R. Susan Foti, M.Ed., L.M.F.T., in private practice in Boca Raton, Florida. "There's a lot of difficulty with communication and differences in expectations and role models . . . and all of this conflict causes a lot of misunderstanding, tension, and frustration."

Communication, and lots of it, is crucial. Only after acknowledging that they are different from previous relationships can the blended family begin to become a new family all its own.

"You need to understand that blending means you don't have to agree with everybody all the time," says Shoemaker. "You can still have your culture, your traditional values. Because you're in a new family doesn't mean you have to forget them."

The point is to blend, not to homogenize.

ing to establish them, on the other hand, there are other issues with which to contend: Jealousy. Insecurity. Fear of rejection. Disappointment. Sexual frustration. Broken hearts. And the loneliness we can feel within a faltering relationship can be more intense than what we'd feel in peaceful solitude. We say that stress is caused by lack of control. Trying to control another human being is not a healthy thing.

Whether your status is single and never married, divorced, or widowed, you'll have stressors with which to contend. But in no case does being alone have to mean being lonely. A chosen family of good friends can provide love, companionship, and support beyond that of blood ties or nuptial vows. "In many instances," says Paul Rosch of AIS, "that's preferable to having to be with relatives you can't stand. You can choose your friends; you can't pick your relatives."

"Strong social support is a very powerful stress buffer, and that is increasingly absent in today's depersonalized society," he continues. "Individuals who can't find that at work or through family ties or friends can do so by joining groups that have similar interests or hobbies, or doing volunteer work, or through religious activities that supply that need. And conversely," he reminds us, "there are people who like that life."

On the Job

We spend more hours on the job than almost anywhere else and more time with our coworkers than we do with the closest members of our family. How well we function "on the clock" impacts

STREET SMARTS

"Don't be afraid to go into your room and cry, to get upset," advises sixteen-year-old Shelly Moyer to others who face the inevitable stresses and strains of acclimating to life in a "blended" family.
"Don't hide it. Don't be afraid to talk about it."

SMART SOURCES

National Mental Health
  Association
1021 Prince Street
Alexandria, VA 22314
800-969-NMHA
www.nmha.org

Visit the NMHA Web
site or call its mental
health information
center toll free for
helpful brochures such
as *Stress and Depres-
sion in the Workplace*
and information on a
variety of mental health
topics at no cost to the
public. Referrals to
local resources are
provided upon request.

our financial and emotional well-being. Our self-worth is often tied up with our career. Losing a job without having another one waiting is one of the biggest stressors there is.

Ironically, the qualities that are most likely to make us successful in the work force—aggression, ambition, drive, and energy—are those which are most likely to hurt us if not channeled in the right ways, according to the National Mental Health Association (NMHA), which lists work overload, personality conflict (especially with superiors), and too much responsibility among some of the most common causes of job stress. The most common symptoms: fatigue, insomnia, high blood pressure, headaches, ulcers, heartburn, inability to concentrate or relax, changes in appetite, and a waning sex drive.

"When a person feels hopelessly overloaded at work, and feels unable to leave job problems behind at night or on weekends, [or] experiences a trapped, immobilized feeling, there is a definite problem," warns the pamphlet *Stress and Depression in the Workplace* (available from NMHA). There's nothing wrong with putting in a few extra hours now and then, but when it becomes a regular habit, think again.

Increased job demands create problems at home for time-starved employees, who then end up feeling too stressed to work effectively. Companies that have traditionally focused on helping solve workers' family problems to better productivity now have to acknowledge that the problems might actually stem from the job.

We're working longer on average—47.1 hours a week, compared to 43.6 hours in 1977; with one third of us bringing some type of work home with us once a week or more, compared with one quarter of workers in 1977. And job insecurities are higher.

Although it's usually those in upper management who are thought to be under the greatest stress, workers at lower levels might have more cause to complain. At senior professional levels, workers often have the advantage of flexibility and the valuable power to remedy the cause of their duress. Others, such as supermarket cashiers or data-entry clerks, don't have as much say—if they have any at all. Research shows that jobs that are perceived as boring and repetitious can pose just as much—or more—of a strain as the job of a high-powered executive.

The most stressful jobs are those that are both boring and time-pressured, like working on an assembly line. When the car manufacturer Volvo gave its workers in Göteborg, Sweden, more flexibil-

Workplace Violence

Researchers at the Center for Crisis Management (CCM) in the School of Business Administration at the University of Southern California found several factors often associated with a high incidence of workplace violence. Among them were employee absences, medical leaves, workers compensation claims, and other health-related factors—factors often associated with stress.

"Our findings validate other research indicating that workplace violence is a pervasive problem," said L. Katharine Harrington, principal investigator of the study, which focused primarily on nonlethal acts, such as threatening phone calls, bomb threats, and fights, the types of violence that occur most frequently in the American workplace. CCM's survey of three thousand human resource and security managers found 43 percent of the survey respondents reporting having experienced some incident of violence in the workplace within the past three years.

F.Y.I.

More than 111,000 violent workplace incidents were reported in 1992, resulting in 750 deaths and a cost to employers of $4.2 billion. Violent crime and mass murders in the workplace almost always stem from job stress.

Source: American Institute of Stress

ity in how they would produce cars, worker absenteeism and blood pressure went down, and job satisfaction went up.

What's a wage-earner to do? You can't just change your boss if his personality gets on your nerves, and, unlike your formula for tolerating crazy Aunt Linda, you can't console yourself with the fact that you'll see him only twice a year. If your office is located next to the social whirlwind of the water cooler—or if you don't have an office—you certainly won't be able to get the corner suite with the great windows on the argument that it will make you feel more relaxed. Uncooperative underlings you had nothing to do with hiring, nasty coworkers, a bad commute, low pay, bewildering new technology with no training to use it, and the inevitable computer glitches all fuel anxiety's flame.

Tips

So much of our workplace situation is out of our hands and depends on the actions and rules of others that even our most constructive efforts or the most sensible solutions are not guaranteed to be welcomed by the powers that be. But by recognizing the main sources of annoyance and at least doing something to better our lot, we stand a chance of kinder, gentler workdays.

• **Take care of yourself.** Good exercise, sleep, and nutrition are vital to every facet of life, and crucial to fighting negative stress. A strong, healthy, well-rested body is better equipped to avoid becoming stressed in the first place, and to better cope with the pressures it does face.

• **Be realistic.** Set reachable goals and deadlines, and plan for them. Think of it as "work triage": break that enormous workload into individual tasks. Do what must be done first, what would be helpful to do second, and leave the extras for last. Tune in to whether you're a morning person or an afternoon person and determine when your coworkers tend to leave you alone and when they're hovering around your desk, and schedule appropriate tasks for the appropriate times.

• **Take your time.** Establish realistic deadlines but also learn to take time off, and use it well. Make sure to get out of the office for a lunch break—walk to the park, around the block, anywhere that's pleasant (and doesn't involve fighting midtown traffic to get to). Stretch your muscles, breathe deeply, relax. Take advantage of coffee breaks; at least stroll to the water cooler. Sitting at the computer for more than a half hour at a time strains eye, neck, and back muscles.

• **Use all your vacation days.** Vacations, be they two-week excursions or long weekends now and again, are essential for refreshing mind and body, and should not be used just to do work around the house. Find a hobby, an interest, a game. Have fun!

• **Choose your battles.** In some jobs the customer's always right; and in almost all of them, for all intents and purposes, the boss is, too. If he's going to hire his nephew, or let his wife cater the holiday party, save your breath. If you disagree with everyone always, or snap at whoever expresses a differing opinion than yours, no one will listen to you and you won't be considered a team player. Save

WHAT MATTERS, WHAT DOESN'T

What Matters

• A calming, renewing home environment to which we can retreat from the rigors of the world.

• Realistic expectations of what we can expect from—and accomplish on—the job.

• Leaving our anger outside the car and off the road.

What Doesn't

• Living up to Martha Stewart or Bob Vila levels of house care.

• Being named Employee of the Year at the price of a broken home.

• Reaching our destinations at a world-record pace while endangering our own—and others'—lives.

Stress Builders and Stress Busters

Stress Builder: "I'll never get this project in on time."

Stress Buster: "If I stay focused and take it one step at a time, I'll make steady progress."

Stress Builder: "My supervisor didn't say good morning. He's probably displeased with my work, and I'll get a bad evaluation."

Stress Buster: "I'm jumping to conclusions. My supervisor may have been in a bad mood. So far all my evaluations have been positive, so unless I get some negative feedback, I'll assume my supervisor is pleased with my work."

Stress Builder: "I can't get my mistake on page 53 out of my mind. The paper is ruined. I have disappointed everyone."

Stress Buster: "No one is perfect. I did my best. I'm overreacting to one mistake when the overall report is fine."

Source: Overcoming Panic, Anxiety and Phobias, Shirley Babior, L.C.S.W.; and Carol Goldman, L.I.C.S.W.; and the Center for Anxiety and Stress Treatment, www.stressrelease.com.

your battle skills for what really matters, and for what stands a chance of being changed.

• **Count to ten.** A first-response reaction to something that angers you often leads to words, actions, and emotions you'll later regret. Give yourself time to regroup. Focus your attention elsewhere, and return to the issue after you've had time to cool down. You will be more productive and effective in the long run.

• **Know your limits.** "Yes people" dig themselves into a hole when they can't live up to their promises. Learn when to just say no and how to do so diplomatically.

• **Coexist with your coworkers.** There aren't many things more stressful than spending extended amounts of time with someone with whom you have a disagreement—be it about the handling of the Feigen account or about the way they finish the coffee and don't start a new pot. When you have a difference, talk it out (face-to-face, in private, and, if possible, on neutral ground). When you just don't like someone, try doing something nice for them. You'd be amazed at the results.

• **Skip the three-martini lunch.** In fact, while you're on the job, skip martinis altogether. "Self-medicating" with alcohol, drugs, or nicotine won't make your problems go away. They'll just give you additional ones.

• **Office sweet office.** You spend as much time there as you spend at home, so it only makes sense to make it comfortable. Whether it's an executive suite or a humble cubicle, your professional space can be made your own. Surround yourself with calming and familiar sights—photographs, cartoons, knickknacks. Put a bowl of potpourri in the corner. Be sure you have adequate lighting and proper equipment to do your work comfortably and well.

• **Don't promise miracles.** If you need more staff, more materials, or more time to do your job, let your employer know. Otherwise you risk what we call "The Rumpelstiltskin Phenomenon": When a miller's daughter weaves a roomful of straw into gold, she doesn't get a bonus—she gets another roomful of straw to weave. Work a "miracle" once, and it often becomes your new standard.

F.Y.I.

The annual cost of job stress to American industry due to absenteeism, diminished productivity, compensation claims, health insurance, and direct medical expenses is $150 billion—more than 15 times the cost of all strikes combined.

Source: WELCOA, *An Introductory Guide for Managers, Supervisors, and Union Members,* Cahill, Landsbergis and Schnall

F.Y.I.

78 percent of Americans describe their jobs as stressful.

40 percent of worker turnover is due to job stress.

60–80 percent of accidents on the job are stress related.

Source: American Institute of Stress

• **Make work friends.** Not even the most sympathetic spouse or the closest friend can appreciate what you endure on the job. A trustworthy confidant with whom you can share and air feelings can help you vent and problem-solve. One caveat: Beware office gossips who thrive on stirring up trouble. And sharing grievances without doing anything about the situation is not the answer, either.

• **Watch for warning signs.** The sooner you recognize you're getting stressed out, the sooner you can do something about it and the easier it'll be to deal with. More and more corporations offer counseling help if things get out of hand. And if you're concerned about this going on the record, get help elsewhere.

• **Consider your options.** If a job is truly stressing you to your limit, think carefully about whether it's the job for you. Is the trouble with the work or is it the workplace? Will a training course help make that computer program more manageable or is the truth that you'd rather work with people than machines. Will you be running away from something you'll only run into again?

Working at Home

WAHM, the online magazine for work at home moms (http://www.wahm.com) asks, "Is every day at your office 'Take Our Daughters to Work Day'? Are there Legos under your desk?"

More than 24 million Americans, according to the American Association of Home-Based Businesses (AAHBB), are opting to leave behind the stresses and strains of the corporate world in favor of working out of their own homes. And the numbers are growing every day.

Home workers might not have to deal with difficult coworkers, interminable staff meetings, the problems of finding day care, or the ardors of a rush-hour commute, but fighting off distractions—from babies who need changing to laundry that needs washing to television that "needs" watching—can be a considerable challenge. The very flexibility that's one of home work's assets can become a liability if it is taken advantage of by other family members on a more tightly proscribed work routine.

"There's a lot of pressure that we put on ourselves, being torn in two directions," says Beverley Williams, AAHBB founder and president. "We have work to do, but we have laundry to do, too. We feel guilty because we're doing one thing and not the other."

Another issue: "While not experiencing the interruptions common to a corporate office," notes the organization, "the home-based business owner may, in fact, feel some stress because of the lack of interruption." Isolation can be hard to handle when you're used to the hustle and bustle of the business world. It was the need to be connected to others, in fact, that prompted Williams to start AAHBB.

Tips

• **Get out.** Get a post office box to force you farther from your home office than your mailbox, meet with clients on a regular basis, and make appointments for some enjoyable lunch hours. Net-

SMART SOURCES

American Association of Home-Based Businesses
P.O. Box 10023
Rockville, MD 20849
800-447-9710
www.aahbb.org

This nonprofit organization's mission is to support home-based businesses at all levels. And it does. A monthly newsletter and tip sheets, including *Stress Management for the Home-Based Business Owner*, are available at no charge to members and for a nominal fee upon request. Visit the Web site or send a self-addressed, stamped envelope for free start-up advice and a tip-sheet list.

work with others who are similarly inclined, and take advantage of the support groups that are springing up nationwide.

• **Establish boundaries between work and home.** Other members of the family might take a while to comprehend that even though you're wearing jeans and sitting at the desk in the extra bedroom, you really are at work, and that you're not ignoring them because you don't love them anymore. Sit down together and establish boundaries of time and space, and far fewer misunderstandings will flare.

• **Have a dedicated work space and schedule.** This will cut down on distractions and interruptions. You can also use the answering machine to screen your calls as another measure to set boundaries.

• **Treat yourself like an executive.** Adapt useful tools for time management, realistic planning, and other life-saving strategies from the corporate world. And don't forget to tell yourself you're doing a good job.

Rage on the Road

In Salt Lake City, Utah, a seventy-five-year-old, angry at being honked at for blocking traffic, followed the "offender" off the road, threw his prescription bottle at him, and then crushed the man's knees with his car. In Maryland, an ex–state legislator knocked the glasses off a pregnant woman after she asked him why he bumped her Jeep with his. In North Carolina, a drivers' education teacher is said to have told a student driver to follow a man who had cut them off, and then the teacher punched the offender in the nose.

And it's not just an American phenomenon. A 1997 *U.S. News and World Report* story noted that "nearly 90 percent of British motorists have experienced threats or abuse from other drivers. Of Brits who drive for a living, about 21 percent report having been run off the road." An Australian study estimates that about half of all traffic accidents in Australia may be due to angry drivers.

Road rage—a deliberate act of violence stemming from a traffic incident—is a worldwide epidemic on the rise. So is aggressive driving: using a vehicle in a way that has less to do with safe transportation than with venting your anger at the world. This means speeding, cutting through traffic, running stop signs, and, in general, endangering (and antagonizing) other drivers on the road.

The incidents that trigger both forms of violence involving drivers are often violations of roadway "etiquette," such as driving slowly in the left lane, honking, tailgating, or changing lanes without signaling. But the underlying cause for our impatience with such seemingly trivial breaches of conduct can often be traced to an accumulation of off-road stress, from the boss's tirade to the credit card company's past-due notice to the kids' temper tantrum last night.

"If you look at the instances of road rage documented by the AAA Foundation for Traffic Safety," says psychologist Mark Lee Edwards, Ph.D., the American Automobile Association's managing director of traffic safety, "you find they're really instances of displaced anger that has nothing to do with driving."

And as Americans are being more pressured and more stressed for time, roads are getting more

SMART DEFINITION

Road rage

A deliberate attempt, prompted by a driving-related incident, to harm someone.

Aggressive driving

Operating a motor vehicle without regard for safety and often resulting in injury, property damage, or violence.

Source: American Automobile Association

How to Avoid the Wrath of Other Drivers

• Don't respond to threats and thereby risk escalating the anger of the hostile driver.

• Avoid eye contact with aggressive drivers.

• Don't make any gestures that might be construed as antagonistic.

• Don't tailgate.

• Use your horn sparingly.

• Don't block passing or right-turn lanes.

• Signal your intentions to change lanes or turn.

congested. "If a driver expects a trip to take ten minutes and it ends up taking more than thirty minutes, frustration grows," says National Highway Traffic Safety Association (NHTSA) Administrator Ricardo Martinez, M.D. "And many drivers will respond to this frustration by acting and driving aggressively, sometimes even after the gridlock ends."

What is to be done about this? The answer can't wait for more roads. "Expansion is often not the answer, or even a viable option," says Martinez. "In short, we cannot always 'build' our way out of the problem."

We have to deal with our attitudes. A community of therapists and scholars has arisen to study the phenomenon and counsel drivers. Their consensus: driving with a good spirit yourself can not only keep you from feeling the rage but keep the ragers from targeting you.

Tips

• **Be sure to give yourself enough time.** "Clocking" your trips instead of enjoying them can result in your seeing any interference—like that slow car in front of you—as a frustration, which can lead to rage.

• **Make your car a good place to be.** Play calming music, keep the temperature controlled, and wear comfortable clothing and shoes.

• **Give other drivers the benefit of the doubt.** If someone tries to get ahead of you, imagine that he or she is on the way to a medical emergency or that the driver has just lost his or her job.

• **Avoid aggressive drivers.** These are the ones who can get your stress levels up.

• **Don't take traffic problems personally.** If you find yourself starting to drive aggressively despite the above, AAA's Edwards suggests three tips to calm down:

1. **Disengage.** If you find yourself in a duel with another driver on the road, leave the scene. Drive slower and let them get ahead of you, or turn off the road.

2. **Distract yourself.** Divert your attention, turn on the radio (to a calming station), talk to your passenger, or look at the passing scenery.

3. **Don't try to blow off a little steam.** Full-blown anger is not easily controlled once it gets loose, notes Edwards. "There's no such thing as letting off 'a little' steam. Once you take the lid from the pot, you just might blow off the top."

Mass Transit Madness

The urban equivalent of road rage, what we've dubbed "mass transit madness" is a rush-hour phenomenon with which too many city dwellers can identify. Even the most mild-mannered receptionist or most civil servant can be transformed into subway samurai under the combined stressors of time pressure, overcrowding, noise, and jostling from the vehicle itself and the passengers in it.

Being crammed into a crowded bus or train makes for a physical intimacy with strangers that you don't share with even your closest friends. The invasion of personal space can make the most innocent gesture appear to be a threat. There's pushing and shoving, hovering strap-hangers, newspapers in our faces—it's not fun.

In most cases, the tension tends to manifest itself in hostile looks or a nasty verbal interchange that can carry its negativity into our workday or home life. In the worst-case scenario, commuters have wound up in physical confrontations or on the tracks. As with road rage, the best offense is a good defense.

Tips

• **Avoid eye contact with fellow passengers.**

• **If you read a newspaper, know how to handle it.** Don't fold your *Times* in someone else's face. If you have to, switch to tabloids for your reading material or stick with books.

• **Become familiar with the words "Excuse me" and "I'm sorry."** Use them liberally.

• **Plan your exit.** Do not wait until the doors are opening at your stop and then suddenly hurl yourself through a crowd to get to them in time. Work your way over gradually.

• **Use the less-crowded front and rear of the train.** Walking a little farther when you arrive at your stop, if safe, has its advantages: both the extra room and the exercise are good for you.

• **Don't answer one aggressive act with another.** If a nasty glance or shove is aimed in your direction, turn the other cheek. Move away if possible.

• **Be safety conscious.** Stand away from the curb or tracks while waiting for the bus or train.

• **Keep your music to yourself.** If you listen to headphones during your commute, turn down the volume so you can hear what's going on around you. Not only will you be better able to stay in touch with your surroundings, but you will also lessen the chance that you'll be annoying your neighbor with unwanted sound. While you're at it, consider peaceful tunes.

• **Give your seat to the elderly or disabled.** You'll both feel better.

• **Leave a little earlier in the morning or later in the evening.** The best way to deal with rush hour may well be to avoid it altogether, if possible.

Being aware of and prepared to deal with day-to-day anxieties can keep them from grating on our nerves, but once- (or twice-) in-a-lifetime occasions call for a different set of stress-relieving skills. Chapter 4 looks at such special events, from weddings to getting a promotion or raise, and answers the question, If it makes us happy, why are we so stressed?

THE BOTTOM LINE

Whatever differences there are between workplace stressors and those within our homes or on the road, taking a positive approach to resolving the negative impact of all types of stress can alleviate a world of strain. Married or single, white collar or heavy laborer, we all experience stress as a necessary part of life and all can learn how to make our lives more relaxed, productive, and enjoyable.

Life Events and Stress

Most of us don't need convincing that difficulties in life are stressful. Losing a loved one or a job, financial duress, divorce, illness, being overloaded with demands or bad news all clearly call upon our coping skills. The truth is, however, many happier occurrences can be stressful as well: getting a promotion or going on the vacation of our dreams; planning or attending weddings, birthdays, holidays, and anniversaries; preparing for and celebrating the birth of a child; and moving into a new home. As much as we celebrate these special events with parties and congratulatory cards, we often find ourselves face-to-face with anxieties in the process.

Not-So-Great Expectations

"People are more likely to [experience] lasting distress from a positive event than a negative event," says psychiatrist Jeffrey P. Kahn, M.D., on the faculty of Cornell University Medical College, and president of WorkPsych Associates, an executive and corporate mental health consulting firm.

An important distinction to make is that good things are not going to make us unhappier than bad things, but the sort of distress they may provoke can be of a more lasting type. Kahn explains: "A positive event creates uncertainty, while a negative event more often creates a loss." The uncertainty, Kahn posits, can continue indefinitely; loss, though painful, has a more predictable end.

It makes sense. Positive events, such as weddings, graduations, and promotions, herald beginnings to what we hope will be continuing happiness and success. Negative events, such as divorces or firings, on the other hand, signal terminations, which, despite all their inherent pain and hardship, have the word "over" built in.

Newlyweds, fresh from the glow of their big day, may harbor fears about whether their marriage will last. And those fears can potentially continue until the day death (or divorce) parts them. A graduate or newly promoted executive, once she's established herself in her swank new corner office, may feel some trepidation over the demands that lie ahead. Divorce, while hardly a party, is an acknowledged hardship that one can recognize as such and work through. Job loss, too, presents undeniable problems to be solved.

"The fears that you *know* are less bothersome than the fears that you *don't* know," says Kahn.

Recognizing stress is also crucial to doing something about it. And it can take us by surprise when it rears its head in connection with happy times. As we've said earlier, the feeling that we've lost control is at the heart of almost every sort of anxiety. And in times of change, when we're entering a new situation with which we're not familiar, a sense of control is often the first thing to go. It doesn't matter whether it's a "better" or "worse" situation, either. What matters is the fact of the change itself, the dimension of the situation that is an "unknown."

When we're facing what we recognize as a negative situation, we're more likely to be on the alert, and so more likely to recognize—and, with hope, become better informed of—the aspects of the situation we need to focus our attention on, and so regain control over.

"It took a long time, but I finally learned that in order to enjoy the dinner parties I'd been throwing for years, I'd have to throw my make-it-perfect anxieties out the window," says fifty-year-old Joan Hill, of Lake Placid, Florida. "I'll never forget the time the oven broke down in the middle of all our preparations and we had to scurry around putting a new menu together—it was actually the most enjoyable event of all."

Lastly, we cannot overlook the great expectations we harbor—and have placed upon us—in connection with such happy events. Often those expectations are based less on reality than on a fantasy scenario woven by Mother Goose and movie producers. The dream wedding. The Norman Rockwell Christmas dinner. The flawlessly decorated new home. Expectations beyond the realm of our particular reality often set us up for impossible goals. Then we feel overwhelmed and overloaded by superhuman demands.

The pressure to be happy is pressure, any way you look at it. And pressure and happiness are an uneasy mix.

Rituals

Blowing out the candles on a birthday cake, gathering for turkey on Thanksgiving, having a white wedding, and celebrating a sweet sixteen are just some of the ways in which our culture marks the passage of time, honors its history, and looks toward its future.

Marking life's rites of passage—the transition from child to adult, single to married, this world to the next—rituals recognize and honor the movement in our lives; and the meaningfulness of the process for those going through them, and the family, friends, and others who make up their "tribe."

"[Rituals] tend to make the event emotionally easier by offering a sort of standard approach," says psychiatrist Jeffrey Kahn.

In its most basic form, ritual reduces the stress of the event by letting us know exactly what it is we can do to observe it. New baby: Cigars. Birthday: Cake, candles, and presents. Marriage: Wedding ceremony, reception, and honeymoon. Twenty-fifth anniversary: Silver. Thanksgiving: Turkey, cranberry sauce, stuffing, and yams. Although we are free (and encouraged) to personalize any and all of the components, if we don't want to make decisions, the steps are clear.

But there's a larger picture to rituals' stress-relieving function: the gathering of kith and kin. Be it a wedding or funeral, the event calls our support group around us, not only to acknowledge but to help us deal with what we're going through. Aunts, uncles, and far-flung cousins we haven't seen in years will gather for a wedding or the birth of a child. Friends will fly in from out of town. And in a day and age when our community—and the stability it used to offer—is scattered from East Coast to West and every point between, these gatherings serve a more important purpose than ever before.

But there's the rub. The fact is, we are not all Waltons, and when family members do not show for an important event in our lives, it can hurt. Other anxiety can surface when they *do*.

"Very often in families there are found rivalries and difficult relationships, and any emotionally charged gathering is going to heighten some of those issues," says Kahn. "In some cases it will reduce some of those issues and in some it will heighten them."

Tips

• **Plan ahead.** Making plans and organizing in advance will free you from tending to last-minute details and allow you to experience the event.

• **Keep your expectations realistic.** If your name isn't John-Boy Walton, don't expect a perfect family reunion.

• **Don't confuse the event with what it symbolizes.** Things can go wrong during the event and not be harbingers of woe for the years ahead.

• **Focus on what *you* want and need.** Other people will be bringing their own expectations and emotions. You handle yours.

• **Enjoy yourself.** If you're the host or hostess, remember to let yourself in on the fun.

• **Feel free to feel stressed.** Anxieties are natural; don't beat yourself up if you're not smiles from head to toe.

Home for the Holidays

'Tis the season to be jolly. 'Tis also the season for stress. The rushing, the conglomeration of personalities, the decorating, the card-sending, the overspending, and the whirlwind of activity associated with many a seasonal observance can obscure the joy of any celebration. Whether it is Christmas, Hanukkah, Easter, the Fourth of July, or simply the thirtieth annual Smith Family Reunion on Flint Hill, anxiety is an oft-in-attendance, if unwelcome, guest.

In the growing number of blended families, no longer is it merely a question of which set of grandparents to visit, but which set of parents to see, with whose children, for how long, and where. "Families that are new, which is what a blended family is, need to take time to develop their own rituals," says Ellen A. Sherman, Ph.D., L.M.F.T., director of the Counseling Resource Center in Boca Raton, Florida. "Where people find that they have pitfalls is that they have not discussed these issues before they got married or before these situations arose. They just assume that because they love each other everything else will work out. Here, more than anywhere else, Murphy's Law comes into play: Whatever *can* go wrong, *does* go wrong."

Tips

• **A few weeks before the occasion, gather the "principals."** Do this in a relaxing environment to discuss what you expect. And everything—from how to celebrate and with whom, to what to eat and when, to where to worship and how—needs to be aired. Don't forget to get children involved, as well: little ones can be invited to choose what color and shape the cookies should be, while older kids can be put in charge of decor. Numerous issues, including budget, gift lists, and the touchier aspects of family politics—like encounters between less-than-amicable ex-spouses—are best ironed out between parents before the children are brought in to keep potential discord from shattering a united front.

• **Expect the unexpected.** Recognize that the best efforts are bound to fall short now and then.

STREET SMARTS

Balanced planning helps avert tension for the Vasquez family in New York City, where two sets of grandparents vie for Christmas morning with little Lizzie and David. "We always visit both," says forty-two-year-old mom Carmen. "But we're sure to alternate whose house we go to first every year."

SMART DEFINITION

First dance

"The 'first dance' happens long before the wedding," says counselor David Sugarbaker, "when the couple agrees that they're fully committed to each other. At that point they begin to consciously or unconsciously establish the patterns of the relationship—with regard to decision-making, communication, conflict-resolution— they will repeat in their marriage. And the first dance determines how the second and the fiftieth are going to go."

• **Take time to remember the occasion.** The point of all the parties and meals and gifts is the celebration of the family and its love.

Do You Take This Stress . . . ?

It can begin with his anxiety over how to pop the question, and whether she'll accept. Or perhaps the tension kicks in on the way to the jeweler, where he discovers the cost of what he'd heard was "a woman's best friend."

For her, a special set of pressures comes into play. "As soon as the announcement is made and the engagement ring is on her finger, she steps into the temporary, specialized cultural role of 'Bride,'" writes David A. Sugarbaker, author of *The First Dance: Engagement's Decisions and How They Shape Your Marriage.* "'The spotlight' is on her, and stays on until the wedding is over."

"It's just as devastating to step out of the spotlight at the end, after the wedding," Sugarbaker adds. "The bride, having performed in a special role and having people react to her in a special way, suddenly finds that no one cares."

What we call postnuptial depression should come as no surprise.

There are emotional upheavals, communication breakdowns, hurt feelings, and differences of opinion; feelings of anger, frustration, worry, and guilt; uncooperative family members, vendors, and contractors; and unexpected obstacles galore.

"A wedding will be stressful for almost anyone, but it doesn't necessarily have to be a problem," says psychiatrist Jeffrey Kahn. "When people have a much harder time, the issues are often more complex. It's not merely the wedding, it's a variety of complicated emotions. The wedding for many people has other symbolic meanings. It can be symbolic of becoming an adult, moving out of the home, and starting their own home."

More important than all the arrangements, all the hors d'oeuvres, is the relationship.

"The bride and groom may think they're arguing about blue or pink ribbons on the rice packets that the guests are going to throw, but they're really negotiating how they're going to handle conflict," says counselor David Sugarbaker. Understanding is more important than agreement. Communicating with respect, support, and love through this high-stress time can establish patterns of conflict resolution that reinforce intimacy rather than create distance; and these patterns can carry over into the marriage.

"We spend a lot of time planning a wedding, and the ceremony is over in twenty minutes, and then we have everything ahead of us," says psychologist Betsy S. Stone, Ph.D., author of *Happily Ever After: Making the Transition from Getting Married to Being Married*. "We spend a lot of time talking about the transitional event and not about what we're transitioning to."

Tips

• **Try not to take things personally.** "The wedding is an emotional event for many of the people there, not just you," reminds Kahn, "and people have greater and lesser abilities of handling those emotions."

• **Take a prewedding honeymoon.** A few weeks before the nuptials, take a break from the planning and remember why you fell in love.

• **Keep your routine as normal as possible.** Maintain a good diet, get plenty of rest and exercise, and don't take on any strenuous tasks beyond those you already have.

• **Ask for help.** Request assistance from family and friends, or invest in a wedding coordinator who can handle all the details.

• **Allow yourself enough time for planning.** Don't let tight deadlines make a hard job harder still.

Baby Makes Three

Follow nine months of the effects of hormonal and physical changes on a relationship with incomparable levels of exhaustion. Then add the responsibility for a fragile, new human life. We hardly need to elaborate on the stress factors of this blessed event.

The arrival of a first child is likely the most physically taxing and emotionally demanding experience either parent will ever undergo. Without the experience accrued by second-, third-, and fourth-time-around parents, the first-timers' worries over this brand new life can lend to the most minor decision a sense of life-or-death panic.

"Is her fever too high?" "Are his cheeks too red?" "Is she eating enough?" The very sudden transition from being experienced adults to being inexperienced parents is a rough one. "Moving from feeling competent and capable to feeling exhausted and ignorant," in the words of psychologist Betsy Stone, can take its toll.

Our perceptions of and expectations surrounding "mommy" and "daddy" roles can compel us into a variety of unfamiliar behaviors and influence our view of both our partners and ourselves. One affects the other until neither parent may recognize the woman or man they'd known and loved before.

"Simply becoming a mother can make your partner uncomfortable seeing you as a sexual object, and women in the rush of hormones post-pregnancy often feel incredibly sexy," says Stone. "What do you do if your partner sees you as a 'mommy' and you want to be a vamp?"

A new father, on the other hand, might feel a great deal of pressure to be strong and competent as "Daddy." The vulnerability he feels—and the support he craves—has no outlet if he's to properly fulfill his perceived role.

Much as we do when we marry, Stone points out, when we have children we make the mistake of focusing on the transition rather than the outcome. We learn how to breathe during labor, but not how to keep breathing for the months and years beyond.

"I remember the inordinate focus on labor and delivery which, at worst, takes forty-eight hours, and it's over," says Stone, "and you have this child for the rest of your life. You don't have to have a whole lot of values or know what you believe in to go through labor. The others you really have to think about. They're harder and scary."

F.Y.I.

Births, marriages, and divorces in the United States in one year:

Births   3,837,000

Marriages   2,390,000

Divorces
granted   1,146,000

Source: Centers for Disease Control and Prevention/ National Center for Health Statistics. Data for the twelve-month period ending with November 1997.

Tips

• **Create and maintain a support group.** Search out other new parents to share what you're going through.

• **Remember that as soon as you think you know what's going on, it changes.** Part of the transition to being a parent is learning to take things in stride.

• **Accept the stressors.** "The problem with stress altogether is that we have [learned to view our stress as indicative of] something being wrong. Stress is indicative of being alive," says Betsy Stone. "The question is 'Is the stress getting in your way?' not 'Should it be there?' The goal then is not to have no feelings, but to figure out how to manage them."

Welcome to the Neighborhood

Almost one out of every five of us relocated in a recent one-year period, according to the Census Bureau. That's about 42 million Americans (16 percent of the population), with 15 percent of them taking up residence in a new state.

And while moving companies, the post office, and local chambers of commerce offer a plethora of helpful checklists and booklets, with more advice than you could fit in an oversized van, few address the emotional anxiety involved.

"Moving triggers a threat to our survival," writes

Arlene Alpert, M.S., L.M.H.C., in *Moving Without Madness: A Guide to Handling the Stresses and Emotions of Moving.* "We can trace it back to prehistoric times when the need for shelter was paramount and meant the difference between life and death."

"It does not even matter if the move is well-planned and looked forward to; in every move there are moments when everything begins to feel overwhelming and out of control."

Beyond the multitudinous details involved in actually getting from here to there are the many uncertainties about what life will be like in the new environment. No matter how well prepared we are, it can be a jolt when we arrive there to learn just how much we have to learn. Not only do we have to acquaint ourselves with our very own new household, deciding what should be placed where, and remembering where things are, but we need to know where to find the supermarket and the doctor's office, the movie theaters and library, the good restaurants and cleaners. And we need to figure out how to get there. There are the administrative hassles of letting people and institutions know you've changed your address, new driver's licenses, registering to vote, and enrolling children in school. The financial strain of equipping a new homestead is not to be overlooked, nor, perhaps, is the greatest hardship of all: finding a whole new set of best friends.

If the relocation has been prompted by a job change, a marriage, or the end of one, there are other emotional issues compounding the move. Such "double whammies" are more and more common. The Employee Relocation Council (ERC), a professional association of organizations concerned with domestic and international employee transfer, boasts a membership of twelve hundred represen-

"I felt like a baby in our new neighborhood," says thirty-three-year-old Brooke Ziggman, who moved from New York to Massachusetts with her husband and children. "I used to know where to go for everything and how to get there, and suddenly I'm a stranger in a strange land. Finally, I just decided to pretend I was a tourist, and tried to make my explorations fun."

tatives from corporations that relocate their employees, as well as nearly eleven thousand individuals and companies from the relocation industry, from real estate appraisers and inspectors to personal counseling and consulting firms. There are even companies that specialize in helping the spouses of the transferees who are on their own while their husbands or wives are busy establishing themselves in new jobs.

"Sometimes we don't anticipate the physical, psychological, emotional, financial, and cultural strain of moving," says David H. Chenoweth, Ph.D., author of *Worksite Health Promotion,* professor of health education and director of worksite health promotion studies at East Carolina University. "We don't anticipate how physically demanding it is, how difficult it is to call all the utility companies and get all the amenities squared away. In another neighborhood, the values, the cultures can be in sharp contrast. People don't see eye-to-eye on things."

Moving is a multiphase process with many more dimensions than can be measured on any floor plan. The best we can do is take a tip from the experienced: Consider it an adventure, and allow a lot of latitude.

Tips

• **Give yourself as much time as possible to plan the move and schedule any activities you want to complete before moving day.** Try to keep as much of your normal routine intact as possible, addressing your physical needs with proper nutrition, exercise, and rest to keep you fortified.

Moving with Kids

• Before the move, look into child-care options, schools, recreation, libraries, and community activities your child can enjoy.

• Include children in the process. Take them on a home-finding trip, and solicit their input on what kind of house they would like to live in. Let the child select and help decorate his or her own room.

• Help children to meet their new young neighbors the first few days after you arrive (but don't present them as replacements for the friends your children have left behind).

• Allow children to maintain contact with special friends after the move via letters, phone calls, or e-mail. If possible, allow friends from the old neighborhood to visit.

• Communicate. Talk to your children about what the move will mean, and listen to what it means to them.

• Keep to your normal routine as much as possible.

• Don't pack away all the familiar favorites (toys, books, blankets, teddy bears); keep a good supply available.

• No matter how busy you are with the move, spend quality time with your children, before, during, and after you arrive at your new home.

• **Get help.** Contact a local moving company or the post office for a check list that will cover everything you have to do and when to do it—from transferring utility services to unloading your refrigerator to getting your pet's veterinary records. And be sure to get references on everyone you hire to reduce worries about whether you can believe what they've said about themselves.

SMART SOURCES

North American Van
 Lines
P.O. Box 988
Fort Wayne, IN 46801
800-234-1127
www.northamerican-
vanlines.com

You don't have to be a
client to request a free
copy of *A Moving Expe-
rience.* Written by a
psychologist who
specializes in working
with children, this
pamphlet helps you
help your children
(from preschool to high
school) adjust to the
move and offers strate-
gies to help adults
cope with their
feelings, including tips
on preventing post-
move anxiety.

• **Allow time for personal good-byes.** Schedule moments with family and friends in lieu of, or at least in addition to, a crowded, going-away blast.

• **Allow yourself grieving time.** "Even though you may be moving on to what you believe is a better life, all relocating families have some sense of grief as they separate from what they have known. You need to accept your feelings and give yourself time to mourn," says counselor Arlene Alpert. "Remind yourself that as you close one door, you open another."

• **Learn about the new neighborhood in advance.** When you arrive there, get involved in your new life. Volunteer work not only benefits the organization with which you are involved, but it helps you take your mind off yourself.

• **Expect to be emotional.** Allow those emotions to surface long after the empty moving van pulls away from your new home. Go easy on yourself, advises Alpert: "Change the critic, the judge, and the victimizer inside your head to a more benign voice."

You're Hired!

Once upon a time, people got gold watches for a lifetime of dedicated work at one job. These days, when an absence of employer-to-employee loyalty has resulted in a workforce that must constantly look over its shoulder and look out for itself, we are encouraged to buy our own timepieces.

"Under the old employer-employee 'social contract,' employees expected to remain with a company for life, or at least over the long term," found the 1997 Employee Loyalty in America Study, a nationally representative survey of more than two thousand employees conducted by the Loyalty Institute of Aon Consulting. "In return for this loyalty to company, workers were rewarded with regular promotions, a few perks, a pension, and increasing salaries and benefits. A decade of downsizing and streamlining has taught employees today that this work life model no longer exists for most workers. In fact, it is estimated that those entering the workforce in the 1990s will change employers an average of six times over the course of their lifetimes." And workers who suffer stress are "significantly less committed" to their firm.

The Loyalty Institute also notes that "anxiety caused by a decade of downsizing has left employees suspicious and cynical about the level of commitment organizations are willing to provide employees."

"The average upper-management people—the VPs and the presidents—are moving to another position or company on average every six or seven years," says worksite authority David Chenoweth. "Many times that involves either relocating or being promoted within the same organization, but both situations present their share of stress."

Losing a job is shattering, but beginning a new one—whether at another firm or via promotion— presents anxieties as well. When you receive a 25 percent raise in pay, and responsibility increases 50 percent, or when you have to work twelve hours a day instead of eight, it's important to ask yourself whether it's a worthwhile move.

For those with new jobs, there are probationary periods, new benefits packages, new keys to a new executive washroom; however, there are also new expectations, new responsibilities, new proce-

F.Y.I.

Number of jobs the average American will hold between the ages of 18 and 32:

Men	8.9
Women	8.3
Total	8.6

Source: Bureau of Labor Statistics

dures, and technology to learn. Entry into a new corporate culture with its distinctive set of politics and personalities involves almost as many adjustments as you'd experience if you'd moved to another land.

No matter how well we do our jobs technically, climbing the corporate ladder involves the risk of an emotional fall or two. Especially after a move from a position in which you are well-established, the adjustment to suddenly being "the new kid on the block" can come as a jolt. You may have to prove yourself to a new set of colleagues who are watching your every move; or you may have to wield authority and provide guidance to people more familiar with the workplace than you are.

Tips

• **Learn as much about the organization and its style of management as possible.** Do your research *before* accepting the job—or promotion (expectations and procedure can vary greatly even among different executive levels of the same firm). Ask other employees what they feel are some of the more common challenges in their world.

• **Arrange an extended visit to get an on-the-job view, if possible.** Is the culture autocratic and dictatorial? Laid back and casual? Is creativity valued or do layers of checks and balances exist?

• **Ask about the most challenging aspects of the work.** Make inquiries of this sort during the interview. What complaints do people have? "Any organization, if they are really employee-oriented, is going to admit that they have some employees who

have legitimate concerns," says David Chenoweth. "If they are not willing to admit that there
are any idiosyncrasies, I'd be questioning whether
I want to work for a company like that."

• **Be realistic.** Especially to yourself and those with
whom you work, acknowledge that you're new, you
have a lot to learn, and you'll be counting on
those with more experience to show you the ropes.
And allow yourself time—it takes several months
or even a year to learn the political situation in
addition to the specifics of your job.

Taking the Work Out of Vacations

Vacation is important. It can revive us, renew us,
refresh our spirit, and restore our sanity. In chapter 8 we let you in on some especially good ones,
and also how to find them, to relax your stress-
beleaguered soul.

But how many times have we felt we needed a
vacation just from planning our vacation? Deciding where to go; finding the time and money to go
there; getting the tickets; finding a room; arranging to have our mail picked up, plants watered,
and pets fed and walked; having our jobs covered
while we're gone . . . the list can be so exhausting
that the time away hardly seems worth the effort.

And when we come back from our time away,
so much work is often waiting for us at the office
that it undoes any relaxation we managed to have.
"Time to pay my vacation penance," one coworker
of ours would moan upon returning to a moun-

SMART MOVE

Steve Loucks, of the American Society of Travel Agents, cites a study showing that 19 percent of people on vacation call their office every day. He's one of them. "If I've been away for a week and not logged on to my e-mail, I'll routinely have a few hundred waiting for me when I get back." His solution on his last vacation: daily half-hour sessions sifting office e-mails from three thousand miles away. "It's sort of a sad price to pay, but it definitely relieves my stress when I return to the office."

tain of paperwork on her desk. "Relaxing is such hard work!"

Our jobs—one of the major reasons we need vacations so badly—are one of the explanations for why we're taking shorter, if more frequent, holidays than the traditional two-week family excursions of years past. "We're finding that the average vacation takes 7.75 days," says Steve Loucks of the American Society of Travel Agents (ASTA), in Arlington, Virginia, "but we're also seeing that a lot of people, especially those in dual-income families, are taking advantage of long weekends to get away."

No small part of the reason for shorter vacations is to avoid paying that "penance." Americans took 70 percent more weekend trips in 1996 than they did a decade earlier, accounting for more than half of all domestic travel, reports the Travel Industry Association of America; of the 604 million weekends away, nearly 80 percent were for pleasure. For many, having to work feverishly for weeks to catch up on their workload is not worth the extra days off.

Again, expectations come into play. We expect so much from our vacations—relaxation, activity, total familiarity with a foreign country, instant revival of our souls—that we stress ourselves out of the possibility that anything will live up to our hopes. We don't take it easy on ourselves.

"The whole idea of taking a vacation is that it is a chance to unwind and regroup," says Joyce L. Gioia, a certified management consultant and co-author of *Lean and Meaningful*, whose masters degrees include both theology and counseling, "and if you don't give yourself the space and time to do that, you're short-changing yourself."

Return from Paradise

Returning from vacation calls for an adjustment as well. Like any big event to which we have been looking forward and planned so hard, post-event blues can and do set in.

If you've been active on vacation, you might need a physical rest; time to adjust to jet lag or the cold after spending time in a Caribbean clime. No matter how much you like your job or household, you might need some time to reconvince yourself that wearing ties serves a function after spending a week in cutoffs and flip-flops; that meals need cooking after surviving divinely on coconuts and mangos straight from the tree.

Where you live can make a difference as well. The heart of Manhattan will present more culture shock after a desert retreat than would a home in the mountains of north Georgia. If you live among horse farms, on the other hand, returning from a Parisian jaunt will call for some reacclimation.

"When I come back from Hawaii I keep looking for palm trees to sit under," says Joyce Gioia, who eases her transition by beginning on the journey home to think about her work and the tasks that need immediate tending to, so "it doesn't all hit me at once."

Tips

• **To reduce postvacation buildup, clear as much as possible off your desk prior to the trip.** Delegate as much responsibility as you can, having a colleague or assistant fill in for you, if possible. Let clients or associates know you'll be out of

WHAT MATTERS, WHAT DOESN'T

What Matters

• Relationships with a significant other, friends, and family.

• Bringing up our children responsibly and ethically, with unconditional love and care.

• Work that's compatible with our life desires.

• A supportive "family" of friends and close relatives.

• Restful, relaxing time off or away.

What Doesn't

• The perfect wedding.

• Delivery-room heroics.

• Higher pay at the price of unhappiness.

• A life that looks like a Norman Rockwell painting.

• Catching up on two weeks' worth of work on the first morning back in the office.

town and tell them who they can turn to in your absence.

• **Return home at least a day before you're due back on the job.** Allow yourself time to wind down, unpack, do the laundry, review your mail, and, in general, reacclimate.

• **Leave a message on your voicemail saying you won't be returning calls until your second day.** Set up a light schedule for the first day or two back in the office, including time for a prearranged "sit down" with a trusted confidant who can fill you in on everything you've missed.

• **Begin switching back to the time zone in which you live.** This may be a difficult one, but do this a few days before coming home.

• **Recognize that it's normal to be tired and out of sorts for a while.** Beyond the emotional adjustment, readjusting our eating, exercising, and sleeping patterns—our body rhythms—makes getting back to normal doubly difficult.

• **Remember that you don't have to work in an office to be struck by post-holiday blues.** If you work at home, schedule a visit to a local museum or cultural attraction to keep the vacation going after you return.

Accepting the reality that anxiety goes hand-in-hand with all manner of life transitions and special events enables us to reduce its impact. In the next chapter we look at how taking better control of our lives can reduce the number of stressors we'll encounter.

THE BOTTOM LINE

Good things can come in stressful packages. As we marry, have children, and move into wonderful, new homes; as we climb the career ladder and take vacations in paradise, we often find ourselves grappling with issues we didn't anticipate facing—including the guilt of feeling less elated than we feel we should. The realities of dreams that come true can take time to adjust to, but, with patience, some practical strategies, and our eyes wide open, such happily-ever-afters stand a better chance.

Managing Your Time and Your Life

No one wants to be a "control freak," but getting a handle on what's out of control in our lives—be it the amount of time available to us, or where we spend it—can go a long way toward relieving stress. A home or office overflowing with excess paperwork or possessions, for instance, burdens us with external stressors that deplete us of our time and energy, leaving us feeling overtaxed, overburdened, and drained. Self-imposed stressors, such as perfectionism, impose demands that can create a spiraling anxiety web. But there is a way out.

Making Time

Everyone gets sixty minutes to an hour, twenty-four hours to a day; and 168 hours to every week. So why is it that some of us are able to sit on our porch swings and smell the proverbial roses, and others can't catch a moment between errands and activities all day?

It's not that the time gods aren't smiling upon all of us with equal favor. The fact is that how we use the amount of time we have available to us is a matter of choice. And the choice is ours.

You Can't Do Everything

Superman and Superwoman imagery aside, one of the sure things in life is that we cannot do—or be—everything, a fact to which we all nod our heads in acknowledgment and yet we persist in believing is not, for us, necessarily true. Somehow, we're the exception. We can be the perfect parent, exemplary employee, best friend, volunteer of the year, Cub Scout leader, bowling champ, home-repair expert, host and gourmet cook all rolled into one.

Wrong.

Although life calls upon us to fill many roles, there are times when some roles must take a back seat to others. On the days when we're a leader in the Cub Scout den, for instance, we can't necessarily be Julia Child or Paul Prudhomme in the kitchen; Betty Crocker or Mrs. Paul will suffice. During tax season, an accountant might have to scratch the bowling tourney off a demanding work schedule. In other words, we don't necessarily have to stop being something, but we might have to stop being so much of it from time to time.

In other cases, we might find we're trying to fill a role or perform a task (or ten) that we'd really rather not. And we don't have to.

Questions to Ask Yourself

• What is it that's compelling you to join every committee at your child's school? Is it because you enjoy being able to make a contribution, or is it because little Adam's mother is on every committee and you don't want to be thought of as "less of a mom" than she?

• Why do you say yes when a coworker asks for help with the annual picnic? Do you enjoy planning large-scale celebrations, or are you afraid that—despite all your past glowing job performance appraisals and yearly reviews—you'll get fired if you don't?

• Why are you going to the bowling alley every Friday night? Do you like to bowl, or does your spouse?

"What you want for your life is as important, if not *more* important, than what others want for you," says Jann Mitchell, "Living Simply" columnist for the *Oregonian* and author of the Sweet Simplicity book series. "This includes your boss, your parents, your children, and anybody else. 'What really matters to me?' is the most important question to ask yourself. Only then can you set priorities and eliminate the stuff that doesn't matter."

Of course, figuring out what we want to do with our time and what we want out of our lives is easier said than done. And identifying those goals, in itself, takes time. Which we don't have. But we have to start somewhere. As we said: we make time for what we want to do.

Tips

• **Jot down how you spend your time.** Don't rely on memory—it can be misleading. Record what you've done over the course of a week.

• **Separate tasks and activities into "have to" and "don't have to" lists at the end of the week.** Going to work or doing the laundry might be a "have to"; running the car pool or ironing the bed sheets might be a "don't have to." Keep quality of life in mind; a "have to" doesn't have to produce concrete "practical" results—it might be spending time with a friend, or reading a bedtime story to your child.

Making the Most of Your Time

These time-compression tips help expand your schedule to allow more room for what you want to do most.

• **Look at frequency:** Do you have to go food shopping daily, or could you get by with a once-a-week trip to the store? By consolidating trips, you'll save transportation time as well as gasoline.

• **Take advantage of proximity:** "Choreograph" errand excursions. For instance, trips to the hair stylist can be combined with a visit to the bank next door, and you can drive through the drug store pick-up window on the way home.

• **Consider simultaneity:** Can you listen to the news in the car on the way to work? Do your dusting while waiting for your facial masque to set?

• **Remember quality:** Fitting less-pleasant tasks into the workweek—say, picking up your dry cleaning at lunchtime—can clear precious weekend hours.

An important caveat: Do not stress yourself out in your efforts to relieve stress—and that includes efforts to save some time. If you find a leisurely trip to the grocery store relaxing, don't rush. If doing too many things at once is the very root of your anxiety, do one at a time. And most of all, don't taint your "want tos" by combining them with "have tos."

• **Double-check your "have tos."** Next to each one, note what you get out of it—a paycheck, clean clothing, a sense of accomplishment, an unexpected compliment. You might find some of your "have tos" aren't necessary. Of those that remain, are they things that indeed have to get done but not necessarily by you? Can anything be delegated or shared? Can a spouse, child, or coworker with more time on his or her hands take over? Can a service person be hired to do the job?

For Louis Brown, getting up an hour earlier has allowed him a leisurely jump on the rest of his day. "That quiet sixty minutes provides invaluable start-up time," says the thirty-two-year-old veterinarian. "Some days I just relax with an early walk during which I think out the day ahead; other times I pay a few bills or do some paperwork before the morning client rush. I get more done during that time than I could accomplish in two hours during the day."

• **Double-check your "don't have tos."** If you don't have to, then why are you doing them? Next to each item, note what you get out of it. You might also find that some of your "don't have tos" aren't superfluous. For an avid golfer, the weekly game might not be a take-it-or-leave-it event; enjoyment is as legitimate a need as our daily bread.

• **Write down how much you enjoy doing each activity.** Rate each in both lists on a scale of one to five, with five being the most gratifying and one being the least so. Starting with the activities that only scored "ones," write down what you'd be missing if you didn't do them. See how many extra hours that adds up to per week.

Clearing room in our schedules is the first step. Deciding what we want to do with our time is another. Looking over the ratings you've given the things that you do will give you a rough idea of the activities that are most fulfilling, but chances are that there are many other things you might want to do that aren't even on the list.

Once you've cleared your schedule a bit, you'll be able to allow yourself time for another list: the "want tos." These might include brunch with a dear friend, a quiet moment in the garden, or that movie you've been meaning to see. Schedule some quiet time to explore your heart and all its desires. Want to learn to play the piano? Change careers? Get into better physical shape? The time to do these things is yours . . . if you take it.

The Problem with Perfectionism

Like being stressed or too busy to breathe, being a perfectionist is a problem our culture admires.

Olympic competitors who train for hours on end every day for years to compete in a seconds-long race are hailed, as are authors on the seventeenth rewrite of a short story, notes Wayne D. Parker, Ph.D., of the Institute for Academic Advancement of Youth at Johns Hopkins University. But there is a difference between healthy striving for excellence and obsession.

In drawing the line between healthy and unhealthy types of perfectionism, two questions need to be asked: (1) Are the goals being pursued realistic? (2) If they are, are they being pursued in a healthy way? According to Parker, one type of perfectionism—an inordinate fear of making mistakes that can actually inhibit achievement—is related to suicidal preoccupations.

"Unfortunately, the same quality that drives some individuals to very high levels of achievement may also lead to their self-destruction," seconds psychologist Sidney J. Blatt, Ph.D., of Yale University, in *American Psychologist.*

Blatt notes that investigators have identified at least three types of perfectionists: (1) Other-oriented perfectionists place unrealistically high standards on those around them—coworkers, family members, and friends. (2) Self-oriented perfectionists put the same level of unrealistic demands on themselves, leaving no room for flaw or failure. (3) Socially prescribed perfectionists believe that others have exaggerated expectations that are difficult, if not outright impossible, to meet; but yet they believe they must meet them to win those others' approval and acceptance. Of the three, the latter two have been linked with a higher risk of depression and suicide.

"Normal" perfectionism, where we derive a sense of pleasure from painstaking effort but are still able to accept limitations, needs to be distinguished from "neurotic" perfectionism, which, writes Blatt, "is driven by an intense need to avoid failure. Nothing seems quite good enough, and the individual is unable to derive satisfaction from what ordinarily might be considered a job well done or a superior performance. Deep-seated feelings of inferiority and vulnerability force the individual into an endless cycle of self-defeating overstriving in which each task and enterprise becomes another threatening challenge."

No matter how well they have done—be it on the job, in a relationship, around the home, or in the classroom—perfectionists can't enjoy a sense of accomplishment; they just keep stressing over how much better they could have done. The impossibly high demands they make upon themselves, and the unrealistic expectations they place on others, can lead only to disappointment, failure, and more stress.

It can be a very tough situation to break out of, especially if we demand to break out of it . . . perfectly.

Tips

• **Set realistic and obtainable goals.** Set these based on your own wants, needs, and abilities, not a superhero's.

Perfectionist's Paralysis

Would you rather be thought of as a person who didn't have the time or as a person who didn't have the ability? For many, putting off a project is a way to hide behind their doubts that they will do a good enough job. Translation: If you didn't do it, you didn't fail at doing it.

"Perfectionist's Paralysis" doesn't mean total immobility; just immobility in regard to the specific task you want done perfectly. In fact, you might keep yourself so busy—with other projects—that before you know it, the day is done and you haven't even looked at the one you were supposed to complete.

"Procrastination is a part of perfectionism," says Bryan E. Robinson, Ph.D., author of *Chained to the Desk: A Guidebook for Workaholics, Their Partners and Children, and the Clinicians Who Treat Them* and *Overdoing It: How to Slow Down and Take Control of Your Life*. "There's a fear of not doing it perfectly or exactly as it should be. If we can't do it perfectly, we can't get started on it."

In *Working Ourselves to Death: The High Cost of Workaholism and the Rewards of Recovery*, Diane Fassel, Ph.D., relates the story of Margaret, whose procrastination stemmed from her belief that she should make no mistakes. "Margaret's perfectionism leads to her procrastination. Her procrastination results in guilt, and her guilt immobilizes her."

Robinson's recommendation for anyone with perfectionism issues: practice doing something imperfectly. "I tell them to leave the bed unmade for a week. They find out they can do it—they didn't die, nobody got put in jail. Some things can be left undone."

• **Remember that your worth as a human being is not dependent upon the tasks you complete, or on how perfectly you do them.** You are valuable simply for who you are.

• **Look less for external approval and more for your own acceptance of self.**

• **Focus on the process instead of the result.** Give yourself credit for just doing the task. In addition, try to learn to take some enjoyment in the process itself.

• **Look for the lessons you've learned from your mistakes.** Take credit for learning them well and trust that making mistakes is one of the most valuable ways we have to learn.

• **Avoid an all-or-nothing approach.** Prioritize tasks into higher and lower priorities, and allocate time and effort accordingly.

• **Look at what you have done instead of what you haven't.**

• **Find one part of your life in which you can be less perfect, and see what happens when you relax your grip.**

• **Recognize imperfection is a human quality.** Realize that being human—and flawed—plays an important role in the healthy, supportive relationships that are so crucial to our overall well-being. Sharing our imperfections with others, and understanding theirs, is part of what friends are for.

Stop Procrastinating

In this success-driven, accomplishment-counting, overworking day and age, many of us choose not to play the game. But some methods of staying sane are better than others. Realigning our priorities, downsizing our "to do" lists, and making sure to take time for ourselves are healthy responses. Procrastination isn't. This very common form of quiet rebellion simply leaves jobs undone, or done late, or simply not done as well. And the stress it produces can wreak havoc with our lives.

When too many things compete for our time and attention, procrastination can take over as a form of self-defense. No matter how simple or easy to do those tasks may be, their sheer volume can have us putting everything off. We don't know what to do first.

Even "overdoers" and workaholics procrastinate. Psychotherapist Bryan Robinson notes that while some work madly to meet self-imposed, unrealistic deadlines far in advance of when the work is actually needed, "Other overdoers postpone what they need to do for fear of not doing it perfectly. They take on too much, wait until the last minute, throw themselves into a panic, and work frantically to complete the task."

For those who have any doubt that the procrastination crisis has reached epidemic proportions, in recent years, the number of Americans filing income tax extensions hit an all-time record.

No one procrastinates about everything. When we really want to do something, we do it. We give ourselves time to do what we need to do, when we need to do it. If you're familiar with the phenomenon of forgetting tomorrow's dentist appointment but remembering a date with a favorite pal that's weeks away, you're familiar with the principle.

If we view procrastination as a symptom rather than as a problem, we stand a greater chance of getting at its root.

SMART MOVE

When you're asked to attend an activity or take on a task: "Listen to your stomach," says "Living Simply" columnist and author Jann Mitchell. "It'll make a noise and turn over if it's something that you don't want to do." First, give yourself time to respond: Say you'll have to check your schedule and will call back. Then, "Get in touch with whether you don't want to do it next week or as long as you live, and [if you're not interested], call them back and say, 'Sorry, I have another commitment.' Do not tell them what that commitment is because they'll use it to convince you otherwise.

"That commitment may be to just staying in your bathrobe all weekend," Mitchell reminds us, "and that's okay."

F.Y.I.

Number of tax
payments with request
for extension of filing
time:

1975	251,118
1985	889,206
1995	1,368,994

Source: Internal Revenue
Service

Tips

• **Check your motives.** Ask yourself why you are doing—or not doing—the task. Will it advance you toward a goal you really want to reach? Is your heart in it? Do you inwardly object to the project ("My better idea was rejected and now I'm supposed to work on his!"), or the person who assigned the task ("Who is she to tell me what to do?")? Sometimes procrastination can be a signal that we can really live without something. Do you really care how shiny your car is, or do you just feel that you should?

• **Unload.** Is your "to do" list burying you alive? Are you burdening yourself with more tasks than can be accomplished in a lifetime of work? If you set yourself up for failure, you're likely to succeed at it. Take it easy on yourself.

• **Do some "task triage."** Decide what needs to be done now, what can wait, and what doesn't need to be done at all. Focus your efforts and energy. Get in touch with what's important to you. We all have our "have tos," but the "want tos" also count.

After you've identified what really does need to be done, a number of techniques can help.

• **Set a realistic deadline.** Leaving the completion of a task open-ended is like saying to someone "Let's do lunch"—unless you set a date, it'll never happen. Say when. And beware of super goals. If the job will take three days, don't promise to have it done by tomorrow. On the other hand, a too-distant deadline can defeat your purpose. Interim deadlines help.

• **One task at a time.** Break each task into smaller tasks. An all-or-nothing approach is a real stress-builder. Doing things a little at a time not only makes them easier to handle but allows you to enjoy a sense of accomplishment sooner.

• **Take the first step.** The journey of one thousand miles really does begin with one step. And the first one can be the hardest. So make it easier on yourself: Just do something. Anything. Turn on the computer. Ease into the task.

• **Remove distractions.** That means people, noise, TV, as well as other things you have to do—including those other tasks you've been putting off. Take the phone off the hook. Close the door.

• **Get physically, emotionally, and mentally ready to work.** Don't let hunger or thirst pull you away from the task at hand. Fortify your body before-hand, and keep a water pitcher or coffee urn within reach.

• **Stock up on your needs.** Beware the unsharpened pencil . . . or unknown phone number, or misplaced tools. Once you're lured away from the task, it's a hard job to return to it, so assemble your equipment. Don't leave yourself excuses to wander.

• **Join forces.** There's nothing wrong with teamwork. Can a coworker or family member get involved? Would a friend enjoy pitching in? You can motivate each other and even have some fun. Two heads, and two bodies, really can be better than one.

• **Get a "sponsor."** Take a tip from twelve-step groups and find someone with whom to check in to be sure you're sticking with the program and help you through the rough spots.

• **Recognize the occasions when delay can be helpful**—when you are tired or angry and cannot concentrate on the task, or when you need more information or equipment. Sometimes things really do look better in the morning.

• **Reward yourself when you get something done.** Acknowledge your accomplishment and give yourself a good pat on the back.

The Up Side of Downsizing, and Other Ways to Simplify Your Life

For most of us, downsizing is a dirty word. It brings to mind jobs lost and finances ruined; it doesn't quite inspire relaxing imagery. But if we can think of it in terms of making our lives more manageable by lowering the number of burdens we carry day to day, downsizing can take on a far more appealing new meaning.

"For a lot of us, the American dream has become the national nightmare," says Jann Mitchell, author of *Home Sweeter Home: Creating a Haven of Simplicity and Spirit.* "Many of us have learned that having more stuff, and bigger and better stuff—houses, boats, cars, clothes—does not really make us happy."

To the contrary. The more possessions, the more files, the more commitments of time and energy we have and accrue, the more firmly we become enslaved to their demands—the arranging and the stowing, the dusting, the appointment-keeping, the finding of it all. We eventually wind up working longer hours to pay for things we won't even be able to enjoy.

In our quest for earthly possessions, we overrun house and home. We store prized belongings; we insure them; we buy alarm systems to protect them; and in some cases we don't even use or wear them for fear that someone might try to take them away. And if bigger, better models come on the market, we start the process all over again.

"I suggest that people make a list of the ten things they prize most, not counting people or pets or photographs," says Mitchell. "Everything else is negotiable. Ask yourself, 'Have I used it in the past year?' 'Do I love this?' 'Does it feed my soul or is it useful?'"

If it would break your heart to throw away grandma's handmade potholder (the one that's so unattractive you've been hiding it in a drawer for years), hold a yard sale. If a yard sale takes too much time, call a local charity and have your donations picked up at your door. You can claim a tax deduction at the same time you unburden your life. And there's always the city dump or recycling bin.

"With everything we can get rid of we're not only freeing ourselves and gaining in time, energy, and space," notes Mitchell, "but we're providing a delightful treasure for someone else to discover."

F.Y.I.

Reduce the amount of junk mail you receive by getting your name off mailing lists. Send each variation of your name (for example, Jane Jones; J. Jones; Mrs. William Jones; Mrs. Jane Jones, and all the other names under which you receive junk mail) and your address to:

Mail Preference Service
Direct Marketing
  Association
P.O. Box 9008
Farmingdale, NY
11735

Director of List
  Maintenance
Advo Inc.
1 Univac Lane
Windsor, CT 06095

Source: Home Sweeter Home by Jann Mitchell

Once we realize we need fewer things, we will find that we need less money to buy them. After "downsizing herself" a few years ago, Mitchell was able to transform her own forty-hour workweek into thirty, and then compress the thirty hours into three ten-hour days.

"Enough is enough when it comes to work, when it comes to stuff, when it comes to activities you don't really enjoy any more," Mitchell continues. "We want to be human *beings,* not human *doings* . . . to recharge our batteries and renew our souls."

Tips

• **Close "the reference library."** Are your shelves and file drawers bulging with information that is too old to be helpful or relevant to the goals you want to achieve? Ask yourself, "Will I ever need it again?" If so, ask, "Could I get it elsewhere?" If so, trash it.

• **Unload.** Stop "contingency keeping"—a term used by Judith Kolberg, head of FileHeads Professional Organizers in Avondale Estates, Georgia, and director of the National Study Group on Chronic Disorganization, to describe a tendency to save every piece of paper we've ever accrued in connection with a purchase, an assignment, or anything we've ever done in our lives, lest we need to prove something to someone down the road. Sometimes it happens when people lose one important receipt or document and don't "recover," says Kolberg. "From then on they have resolved to hold on to everything forever. Well, forever is a long time—it takes up a lot of space."

• **Bring in an objective pair of eyes.** Enlist a good friend who can be a bit less sentimental about that old basket of seashells and the dried-out bouquet. If it really hurts to part with, keep a photograph of the object as a memento.

Learning to Say No

"Just say no" is another easy piece of wisdom that can be difficult to put into practice. And not just for teenagers fighting off drugs.

Turning down some responsibilities, tasks, even social activities, no matter how filled our calendar is, can be difficult. The expression: "If you want something done, ask a busy person to do it" rings true. Such "doers" often won't hesitate to take on another task, another committee leadership, another meeting, another demand on their time and energy. How else to keep all the world thinking of them as competent and willing to help?

For the altruists among us, there's another way of looking at it. "Each time we say no we create an opportunity for someone else to rise to the occasion, accomplish that task, and feel immensely good about themselves," says Jann Mitchell. "So we're acting nobly, which has 'no' at the beginning of the word."

The Chronically Disorganized

The "organizationally challenged," who have been disorganized the majority of their adult lives, for whom self-help efforts have failed, and who don't see a day go by without a misplaced key, a forgotten appointment . . . "Chronic disorganization is not a medical thing," says professional organizer Judith Kolberg, director of the National Study Group on Chronic Disorganization. "We don't cure it, diagnose it, twelve-step it, or medicate it. It's a quality-of-life issue."

Organizing Strategies to Help Clear Your Mind

Organization encompasses much more than just nicely arranged desk drawers or an alphabetized spice rack. It's a method for putting time to its best use, running a meeting well, and thinking clearly, for starters. Bringing order to our physical world can provide a great jump-start to relieving a lot of mental clutter.

Disorganized space is space that's out of control. When we can't find something quickly and easily, we are, essentially, being challenged by our surroundings. And that's a battle we can do without. A buried calendar, for instance, or one that's cluttered with all manner of indecipherable notes, presents obstacles to every commitment you've made.

"All of a sudden you have that sinking feeling that there was a deadline you forgot about, or someone you were supposed to call, but because you didn't have a system to remind you, that falls through the cracks and tarnishes your reputation," says Stephanie Denton of Denton and Company, and also on the board of directors of the Austin, Texas–based National Association of Professional Organizers.

A desk piled with papers can hide the important bill we were meaning to get into the mail, or the letter that we needed to answer posthaste.

"We get more mail in one week than our parents got in a year, and more mail in one year than our grandparents got in a lifetime," says professional organizer Judith Kolberg. "That's scary."

For those who have their own method of organizational madness (the closet or desktop is overflowing and chaotic, but they really do know where everything is), drawbacks can arise when the need to enlist someone's assistance comes to pass. Even if we know that the file we need is the one marked not with a label, but with a coffee stain, we can't count on others to appreciate our system, and so we're limited in our ability to bring in help.

And don't let visions of perfectionism—those photographs of militarily precise pantries or closets or painstakingly detailed organizer entries—intimidate you.

"I'm a professional organizer, not a perfect organizer," says Denton. "I would never want someone to feel like they had to live up to a perfect standard, because it's not about being perfect, it's about making it work for you."

Tips

• **Give yourself time to organize.** Set aside a few moments at the start and end of each day for maintenance: filing, updating, paying bills.

• **Keep it simple.** "Be as organized as you need to be," says Judith Kolberg. Resist pressure to buy the newest electronic organizer or the agenda with a thousand sections. Fancy can be confusing. Don't keep superfluous systems, and use the ones you have consistently.

• **Use an appropriate system.** We all think and work in our own way. Some of us love elaborate methods of categorization and others work better with simple to-do lists. Customize purchased orga-

SMART SOURCES

National Association of
  Professional
  Organizers
1033 La Posada
Suite 220
Austin, TX 78752
512-206-0151
www.napo.net

With more than one thousand members, this nonprofit organization provides referrals to professional organizers in your area with a wide range of specialties, from office or home management to student or elderly concerns. Fees generally range from fifty to several hundred dollars, depending on the area of the country and the nature of the work.

SMART SOURCES

Feng Shui Institute of
   America
P.O. Box 488
Wabasso, FL 32970
561-589-9900
www.windwater.com

The first organization
of its kind to teach a
feng shui certification
course for profes-
sionals, FSIA offers an
international referral
service by phone or on
its Web site.

nizer systems by removing unnecessary sections or creating your own.

• **Choose your tools wisely.** Don't confuse technology with organization. "Technology is not a substitution for organization," says Stephanie Denton. "Technology is just another tool, like a file cabinet or a three-ring notebook. You have to have the tools that are right for you."

• **Get help.** If things are really out of hand, consider hiring a professional organizer, who can do anything from helping you determine an appropriate system and the right tools to manage it to managing the system for you with periodic check-up visits. Be sure to check references.

Feng Shui: Interior Designing a Calmer Life

A peaceful home—one in which we can relax and recuperate from the challenges of the world outside—can provide a comforting embrace at the end of the day. Calm colors, welcoming sofas and chairs, warm, gentle lighting, and aesthetically pleasing surroundings can soothe the most savagely stressed of us all.

One approach that has lately been enthusiastically lauded by a raft of otherwise fast-living celebrities and business leaders is born of ancient roots. Feng shui (pronounced *fung shway*), the Chinese art of putting an individual in harmony

The Colors of Feng Shui

Adobe: Reflects connection.

Blue: Expresses self-esteem and mystery.

Cobalt: Connects one to a higher purpose.

Gold: Expresses abundance.

Green: Expresses expansion and growth, and promotes tranquillity.

Lavender: Allows freedom from cravings.

Light green: Wistful of the past.

Lime: Awakens the spirit.

Magenta: Sparks higher mental, emotional, and spiritual processes.

Orange: Inspires fusion.

Powder blue: Invites contemplation.

Purple: Reinforces supremacy.

Red: Ignites, stimulates.

Saffron: Kindles love.

Tan: Turns us inward.

Terra cotta: Strengthens security.

Turquoise: Deepens ecstasy.

Verdigris: Deepens commitment.

Yellow: Clarifies.

Source: Feng Shui in the Garden, by Nancilee Wydra, Feng Shui Institute of America

with his or her surroundings, takes both inner and outer nature into account.

Good feng shui (the literal translation: "wind water") has been credited with bettering health, stamina, mood, spirituality, prosperity, even fertility by manipulating ch'i or qi (pronounced *chee*), a metaphysical life force, to flow smoothly, within our bodies or where our bodies live or work.

"Feng shui is the art of understanding how each of us is affected by the places we inhabit," writes Nancilee Wydra, founder of the Feng Shui Institute of America (FSIA), in *WindWater,* the organization's newsletter. "If you can identify con-

WHAT MATTERS, WHAT DOESN'T

What Matters

• Knowing how to say no.

• Delegating whatever you can.

• Recognizing your own goals and objectives so you can plan a course to attain them.

• Doing your best.

• Creating a peaceful home environment.

What Doesn't

• Doing everything.

• Keeping control over everything yourself.

• Busyness for busyness's sake.

• Doing things perfectly.

• Fitting into someone else's idea of a peaceful home environment.

ditions in a home or office that could be detrimental to functioning at optimum, you can make adjustments and tip the scales in your favor to achieve what you desire."

"Our homes and offices don't have to look like Chinese paintings," says Jami Lin, author of *The Feng Shui Anthology: Contemporary Earth Design.* "Feng shui concepts can be applied to any design style."

With the correct shape, color, composition, and placement of the structures and objects around us, we can channel ch'i in the right ways through the specific "energy centers" that influence particular aspects of our lives.

"Nature is perfect and if we design our environment with her as a model, then we are part of nature's flow," says Lin. "When we're in harmony with nature, we're in harmony with ourselves. If we're in harmony with ourselves, stress doesn't exist."

Feng Shui Dos and Don'ts

Many feng shui practitioners blend the ancient Chinese traditions with their own. In Brighton, England, the Feng Shui Association incorporates a "mystical tantric" (Tibetan Buddhist) approach for "better balanced coverage." Lin's "Earth Design" takes contemporary Western life into account for a sort of "feng shui plus." Nancilee Wydra, founder of the Pyramid School, established the Feng Shui Institute of America, "where Eastern philosophy meets Western sciences." Here are a few suggestions from several schools of thought.

• Don't keep bonsai trees (there's no stunted growth in nature), cut or dried flowers, or caged pets indoors.

• Arrange your garden with red and yellow flowers in a flowing pattern; adding evergreens on the property line will secure longevity. Don't plant anything to obstruct the front or the back of the home, which would block the good ch'i. Do remove any dead plants or trees, and anything with thorns.

• Hang wind chimes and bells in dark corners and long corridors to attract and invigorate ch'i.

• Don't leave bathroom doors open, allowing ch'i to flow down the drain.

• Discard anything you do not find beautiful, functional, aesthetic, or positive; it's thought to hold negative energy.

• Always enter your house through the front door, rather than the garage or kitchen areas, which are reminders of work, rather than calm.

• Don't have a long driveway leading straight to the front door. The longer a path, the more intense the ch'i flowing along that path becomes. While ch'i is good for a building's feng shui, very intense ch'i is "like an arrow piercing the structure."

• Don't have a visually unobstructed interior path from the front door to the back door: It allows ch'i to flow through the house too quickly for you to reap its benefits.

• If you have a staircase directly facing the front door, hang a distracting crystal above the door to keep ch'i from coming down the stairs and going straight out of the house.

• Use earth tones and representational figures made of ceramic or clay to help reduce stress and to better ground good energy.

While tending to our physical world can set the stage for mental and emotional calmness, putting our minds at peace can reduce our susceptibility to those areas of the world beyond our control. From meditation and prayer to laughing and crying, chapter 6 explores some of the ways we can do just that.

THE BOTTOM LINE

Managing our time; reducing the demands placed upon ourselves; clearing up the physical and mental clutter with which so many of us grapple; and making our home environment a sweeter place are just a few of the ways in which we can take control of our lives and reduce the stress in them.

Putting Your Mind to the Task

In chapter 5 we explored the ways in which we can reduce our stress levels by reducing the number of stressors in our lives. Here we focus on how to reduce our stress levels by reducing their impact upon us: by expressing our feelings through laughter or tears; by calming our minds through meditation and prayer; by using biofeedback to gain control over our physical responses; and even by taking our gender into account.

Learning to Let Go

"Don't let it bother you." "Take your mind off it." "Forget about it." "Don't worry." "Let it roll right off your back."

But how?

Numerous studies have proved the effectiveness of "behavioral medicine interventions"—relaxation techniques that include meditation, prayer, creative visualization, and deep breathing (some covered here, others in later chapters)—to help us arrive at a calmer state.

Herbert Benson, M.D., founder of the Mind/Body Medical Institute of Harvard Medical School and chief of the Division of Behavioral Medicine at the New England Deaconess Hospital, has coined the term "relaxation response" to describe a "counterbalancing mechanism" to the body's fight-or-flight response.

"Just as stimulating an area of the hypothalamus can cause the stress response," he writes in *The Wellness Book,* "so can educing the stimulation result in relaxation." The result: slower breathing, untensed muscles, untroubled thought.

In other words, while anxiety and stress increase heart rate, blood pressure, breathing rate, metabolism, and muscle tension, relaxation can reverse the impact of anxiety and counteract its harmful effects.

You may have experienced this effortlessly as you were lying on a beach in the Caribbean, or basking in the warm glow from the fireplace after a day on the slopes, or collapsing on the couch after returning home from the rush-hour traffic jam. But there are ways to elicit the response even in the midst of stressful events. Deep breathing, meditation, stretching, imagery, muscle relaxation, and repetitive exercise and prayer are some of the techniques that help.

Meditation and Prayer

Whether with the aid of a mantra or by a candle's flame, whether done in conjunction with physical movement or confining the "motion" to the mind, meditation and prayer have for thousands of years been bringing their adherents a sense of peace they hardly needed science to verify.

Researchers now believe some of the physical benefits of meditation may be due to its effects on cortisol, a stress-linked hormone that, when chronically produced, can inhibit the immune system and slow tissue repair. Meditation may slow or reverse this process. Studies of people taught transcendental meditation (TM) showed that the subjects had cortisol levels 15 percent lower than before they had begun practicing meditation. Another study found that long-term practicers of meditation had a drop in cortisol levels of nearly 25 percent.

SMART MOVE

Spiritual relief of stress is hardly a new concept. "Rejoice in the Lord always," exhorted the apostle Paul to the church at Philippi as early as 53 A.D. "Do not be anxious about anything, but in everything, by prayer and petition, with thanksgiving present your requests to God. And the peace of God which transcends all understanding, will guard your hearts and your minds in Christ Jesus."

A study published by the American Heart Association in the journal *Hypertension* showed that transcendental meditation can significantly lower blood pressure, to an extent commonly found with antihypertensive drugs.

"Our findings indicate that the use of the stress-reducing TM technique by itself—independent of one's lifestyle or stress level—decreases high blood pressure," said psychologist Charles Alexander, Ph.D., a coauthor of the study. "This is critically important because research shows that people who are high in psychological stress (that is, anger, depression, anxiety, and low self-esteem) generally find it difficult to initiate and maintain lifestyle changes, typically reverting to at-risk behaviors after some time."

In addition to transcendental meditation, religious belief and faith are prompting "amens" from many in scientific community. All types of spirituality are being looked to for their physical benefit.

"I'm not saying that physicians should supplant clergy or that prayer should supplant Prozac," said Dale A. Matthews, M.D., of Georgetown University as quoted in *USA Today*. But Matthews does "believe that physicians can and should encourage patients' autonomous religious activities."

At the 1997 meeting of the American Association for the Advancement of Science, Matthews and other researchers presented evidence of the positive influence of religious belief on health. A review of 212 studies found three out of four studies showing benefits.

One theory: much like meditation, prayer and ritual may slow the production of stress hormones in the body, as well as relieve high blood pressure, insomnia, and infertility, among other afflictions with which stress is linked.

A Duke University study of the elderly found that those who attended weekly church services were 50 percent less likely than nonattenders to have high levels of the protein interleukin-6, associated with illnesses such as Alzheimer's, coronary diseases, and osteoporosis.

The social support and friendships that church attendance confers via both services and other activities are undeniable blessings when it comes to alleviating the anxieties of life. But a Dartmouth heart-surgery study found a six-month survival rate three times higher in those who derived "strength and comfort" from religion after researchers screened out the socialization component.

Church attendance, in fact, isn't a requirement when it comes to bettered health. The meaning, purpose, and greater self-satisfaction found in the lives of the spiritual, regardless of how their spirituality is practiced, has been theorized to reduce stress in and of itself.

Even after taking into account lifestyle factors, such as churchgoers' lower alcohol and tobacco use, and the benefits of social contact, the health benefits remained significant.

Then there are other possibilities: one San Francisco study randomly divided 393 seriously ill heart patients into two groups. Half were prayed for, half were not, and none knew which group they were in. The prayer recipients suffered fewer health complications.

Learn to Relax

Once or twice a day, set aside ten to twenty minutes of private time to replenish your spiritual energy, and practice the "relaxation response."

F.Y.I.

The number of American medical schools offering courses on spiritual issues has risen from three to more than forty in the past three years.

Source: Consumer Reports on Health, July 1998

1. Get comfortable and eliminate any potential disturbances. Do not let furnishings, constrictive clothing, hunger, heat or cold, or a ringing phone distract you.

2. Close your eyes, or focus on a pleasing image.

3. Repetition of a single word, phrase, or sound—for instance, "peace," "the Lord is my shepherd," or a gentle hum—will help focus your mind away from daily cares.

4. Relax your muscles, and breathe slowly and naturally, repeating your chosen word or phrase as you exhale.

5. Don't stress out over this. If your thoughts wander, just guide them back.

Tuning In to Our Selves

Another approach to learning to relax allows us to actually "see" how we're doing, and so help us to do it better. Biofeedback operates on the premise that by becoming aware of involuntary bodily changes and functions, such as heart rate or muscle tension, we can bring them under our control, and better our frame of mind along with our physical health. The technique is used to treat a long list of stress-related conditions such as migraine, hypertension, and insomnia, as well as many other maladies of body and mind, from attention deficit disorder to incontinence.

"Biofeedback is so effective that our nation's government and the military uses it to train individuals to reduce stress and stay well," according to Rob Kall of the Association for Applied Psychophysiology and Biofeedback (AAPB). "The bottom line is that biofeedback offers a treatment that lasts long after the symptoms are gone, providing self-control skills patients can use for the rest of their lives to feel good and live better."

According to AAPB, the term "biofeedback" was adopted in the late 1960s to describe lab procedures initially developed in the 1940s that trained research subjects to alter their brain activity, blood pressure, muscle tension, heart rate, pulse, and other internal activities of which we're normally not consciously aware. With a biofeedback monitor providing auditory or visual information about what is going on inside the body, the theory holds, we can attain a true reading on physical reactions and processes formerly thought to be beyond our reach.

For instance, a monitor might flash a light or sound a beeper whenever the small muscles in the head and neck area tense, a common cause of tension headaches. To relax the muscles—and avoid or reverse the headaches—you would need to slow or stop the flashes or beeps.

Although this may well sound like putting the cart before the horse, it nevertheless has been shown to work. With practice, we learn to associate sensations from our bodies with levels of tension, and so learn how to relax them (and the rest of us) on demand. And no, we don't need to stay "hooked up" to do so: Once we learn the technique, research shows, we will be able to do so with no sensors attached.

There's another advantage to using this stress

SMART SOURCES

Association for Applied
  Psychophysiology
  and Biofeedback
10200 W. 44th Avenue
Suite 304
Wheat Ridge, CO
  80033
800-477-8892
303-422-8436
www.aapb.org

Upon request, this national professional organization will provide free referral to member practitioners in your state (AAPB membership does not imply certification), along with fact sheets on certification criteria; tips on how to chose a practitioner; and the booklet, *What Is Biofeedback? How Does It Work? How Is it Used?* When contacting AAPB, specify the type of practitioner that you are seeking; for instance, you might want one familiar with stress management techniques.

management tool: not only do the machines detect our internal goings-on with far greater sensitivity and precision than we are able to on our own, but sometimes technology can help when human support or counseling will not.

"Paradoxically, it's somewhat comforting, for some people, to be relating to a machine rather than a person," reports James A. Manganiello, Ed.D., of the New England Mindbody Institute in Cambridge, Massachusetts. The institute regularly incorporates biofeedback techniques in all its approaches to stress-related maladies. "Some folks find that getting information from a computer is less threatening."

Tips

• **Check with your health insurance company.** Some providers accept biofeedback therapy as a treatment method for an increasing number of health-related problems and will reimburse some or all of the costs.

• **Ask the practitioner whether he or she is certified; if so, by which organization.** The Biofeedback Certification Institute of America, which includes stress management as one of its areas of specialty, is one of several such organizations.

• **Look for a licensed health-service provider who has more than technical ability alone.** Certification and training on the equipment is important, but so are counseling skills. "Too often, the assumption is that you don't have to work with the personality," says James Manganiello, a licensed clinical psychologist. "I get anxious about people trying to get rid of their symptoms without pondering what the symptoms have to say about what's going on in their lives."

• **Use the appropriate approach to target your specific problem.** Learning to relax head and neck muscles, for instance, might be the answer for those whose stress manifests itself in tension headaches, but it might not be the most effective treatment for those whose anxiety shows up via an elevated heartbeat; these people are better off learning to slow their pulse.

Laugh When Your Heart Is Stressing

"When we are going through hard times, we say, 'Someday we will laugh about this.' I say, 'Why wait?'" says Joel Goodman, Ed.D., founder of the Humor Project in Saratoga Springs, New York. "In a world filled with change and transition, humor is a great way to help us keep our balance."

If the sheer pleasure of a good laugh is not enough to convince you of the healing power of humor, there's science to back up the serious physiological benefits of a lighthearted lifestyle. Over the short term, studies have found, a hearty guffaw can result in lower post-laugh blood pressure levels; a good belly laugh can "massage" and relax muscles from face to abdomen; a healthy chortle can prompt the brain to release stress-reducing endorphins; and a knee-slapper can temporarily boost levels of virus-fighting immunoglobulin A. Research confirms that laughter has an effect on

SMART MOVE

Biofeedback can be a useful adjunct to psychological counseling. We might not be consciously aware that, say, our spouse's new job makes us feel anxious, but if our blood pressure increases whenever the topic is mentioned, our body is letting us know it might be worth a look. "If I chronically perceive things in stressful ways, I want to modify those patterns," says James Manganiello, of the New England Mindbody Institute. "By learning to recognize something that's disturbing, and learning how to relax deeply when it is triggered, you can avoid becoming possessed by its stress-inducing point of view."

SMART SOURCES

American Association
  for Therapeutic
  Humor
222 South Meramac
Suite 303
St. Louis, MO 63105
314-863-6232
www.aath.org

The Humor Project
480 Broadway
Suite 210
Saratoga Springs, New
  York 12866
518-587-0362
www.humorproject.com

These organizations
dedicated to furthering
the knowledge of
humor and laughter as
they relate to healing
and well-being are
good for scientific literature . . . as well as
punchlines.

most of the body's major physiologic systems. Even major hospital centers have in-house humor TV channels and clowns on staff.

In the long run, a good-humored outlook on life can not only better our physical well-being but markedly reduce the self-inflicted pressure which adds to any external stressors we may face. It simply betters our morale and quality of life. And that's no joke. Just ask the American Association for Therapeutic Humor.

Humor relieves anxiety, as can be almost palpably felt when an amusing comment cuts through a tense situation. (Think of "nervous laughter" as involuntary self-defense.) Humor helps us cope, taking "power" away from the things that stress us. In Gail Sheehy's book *Pathfinders,* the ability to see humor in a situation was a favored coping device of men and women who have found constructive ways through major life crises. Norman Cousins's *Anatomy of an Illness* legitimized the role of humor in recovery from physical illness.

"It's real important to be serious about our work, our parenting [and other areas of responsibility]," says Joel Goodman, "but it's equally important not to take ourselves too seriously. The gift of being able to laugh at yourself is a godsend. We need to be in search of excellence, but it's crucial that we not become saddled by the yoke of perfectionism. That's where the gift of laughing at ourselves comes in."

"In today's fast-paced society, every professional is faced with some degree of stress," says therapeutic humorist Karyn Buxman, R.N., M.S., on her HumoRx Web site, "and whether the source of stress is at work or at home, the results can be costly. But laughter is the best medicine."

Tips

• **Surround yourself with the stuff smiles are made of.** From cartoons and jokes on the refrigerator to Slinkies in your briefcase, these treats can help lessen a hard day.

• **Take laugh breaks.** When things are getting too heavy, or a situation seems to be getting out of control, switch gears for a while.

• **Forget the punchlines.** You don't have to be Henny Youngman or Joan Rivers to add more laughter to your life. "Humor is an attitude, a set of skills, a way of dealing with life that goes beyond joke-telling," emphasizes Goodman. What it has more to do with is an approach to life, a mental flexibility that will let us roll with the punches that life throws—considerable comfort for the many of us who can't deliver a one-liner in fewer than ten paragraphs.

• **Choose your laughter.** Everyone's sense of humor is different, and it changes by day and by mood. Collect your own humor library: books, newspaper columns, a folder of favorite cartoons, amusing advertisements, the typos in your boss's last memo—anything that brings a smile.

• **Keep a cartoon on your bulletin board.** Alternatively, if your workplace isn't quite Barnum & Bailey's (or maybe because it is), you might have to be on the discreet side; there's always the desk drawer.

• **Let it out.** Humor is a safe way to take the edge off anger, and, for some of us, it's easier to share fears or worries when they're couched within the confines of an amusing anecdote.

Cry Out Loud

We do it at weddings and funerals, in airports and movie theaters, at home and on vacation, when alone and with friends. We do it when we're feeling depressed, when we're too happy for words, and when a joke is particularly good.

But as common as crying may be to all of us, it can carry a social stigma nevertheless. We apologize for shedding tears and try to hide when we do; and if others see us crying, the first thing they do is try to help us stop.

Many of us, however, may be better off if we keep the tears flowing. Not only can crying help us feel emotionally relieved, but it may improve our physical health as well. Like laughter, tears are a natural way for the body to reduce anxiety, let out negative feelings, and recharge.

When Margaret T. Crepeau, Ph.D., of the University of Pittsburgh, compared men and women with the stress-related disorders of ulcers or colitis with healthy subjects, she found those with the stress-linked ailments more likely to see crying as a sign of weakness or loss of control. Many in the study reported that when they were unable to cry or repressed their tears, their illnesses worsened. Other findings suggested that high blood pressure, arthritis, and tension headaches, among other conditions, could also become more severe when emotions were suppressed.

Technically speaking, humans "cry" constantly. Cleansing tears, secreted by lachrymal glands in the eyes' upper corners, are carried across the eye whenever we blink, automatically adjusting the lubrication as needed—for instance, by increasing tears to ease irritation from dust or fumes. These lubricants contain antibacterial enzymes that may also fight infection.

Tears shed in response to strong emotion, on the other hand, are prompted by the brain's limbic system, which sends a message to the hypothalamus to activate the tear glands. Emotional tears are chemically different from those shed in response to, say, dust. They contain more protein, as well as stress-induced chemicals, including various hormones, a class of catecholamines that includes adrenaline, and possibly beta-endorphin, one of the body's natural pain relievers. By crying, in other words, we almost literally release the tension associated with stress. Studies continue to explore variations in tears of joy, laughter, anxiety, grief, depression, and anger.

High levels of anger are known to have a negative impact on patients with heart disease or hypertension. One report found heart-attack patients far more likely to suffer a second attack if they tended to keep their unhappiness inside. The theory is that when patients bottle up negative emotions, the body becomes physically stressed and the brain overproduces hormones that can weaken the heart.

Just as each one of our tears differs from every other chemically, crying patterns vary from person to person. William H. Frey II, Ph.D., author of *The Mystery of Tears*, studied monthlong "crying diaries" of several hundred volunteers. His findings: Sadness accounted for one of every two crying episodes, happiness for one of every five. Anger caused 10 percent of all tears; sympathy, 7 percent; anxiety, 5 percent; and fear, 4 percent.

WHAT MATTERS, WHAT DOESN'T

What Matters

• Finding the time for peaceful reflection.

• Using biofeedback to tune in to what your body's telling you.

• Lightening up your life with a smile.

• Expressing your emotions.

• Doing what you need to do to take care of yourself.

What Doesn't

• Meditating or worshipping "by the book."

• Using biofeedback without a thought as to why you're feeling the stress that causes physical change.

• Covering up tension for the sake of a calm demeanor.

• Limiting your options to the boundaries of cultural stereotypes.

Tips

• **Have a good cry.** If you feel tears welling up—for whatever reason—let them flow out of your body along with the stress hormones they contain.

• **Don't stifle your calls for help.** If you don't cry, you might miss out on the opportunity to communicate your feelings to someone who could offer emotional support.

His Stress, Her Stress

The way we see stress—and the ways in which we react to it—has a lot to do with whether we're seeing it through male or female eyes.

For one thing, our bodies don't react to stress in the same ways or to the same extent. Research at Duke University found that, on average, the blood vessels of women constricted less under stress than did those of men. The greater the constriction, the higher the blood pressure, which may account for the greater prevalence of stress-linked hypertension and the coronary disease associated with it, in the male population. The "female" hormone estrogen, it is theorized, might have a protective effect against certain maladies.

Studies have also shown a relationship between job stress and gender. While men's blood pressure tends to be elevated at work and on the job, returning to lower levels when they return home, women's blood pressure remains elevated even after hours.

"One of the explanations for this phenomenon," says James A. Blumenthal, Ph.D., professor of medical psychology at Duke, "is that women have a greater total workload. They work their pay job, and come home and work their unpaid job."

On various other measures of stress symptoms, including heart-rate responses and subjective evaluations of what causes anxiety, women tend to score higher than men as well. "Whether this means simply that women are more sensitive and aware and willing to report these symptoms than men, or actually have more symptoms has been debated," says Blumenthal. "It's probably a combination of both: They're more willing to recognize and admit to stress."

Women are also more likely to express their feelings and seek support, lessening the harmful impact of their anxiety. In William Frey's crying-diary survey, the differences between men and women were pronounced: Only 6 percent of the female respondents reported no emotional tears compared with almost half the males.

Hormones that help regulate tear production may provide a physical explanation for at least some sex-based differences, Frey posits, but cultural values have an undeniable impact on the differences in crying patterns between men and women. For men, any show of emotion is seen as a sign of weakness; whereas some researchers have gone so far as to credit women's freedom to vent with the female gender's longer life spans.

Learning to express our emotions is a powerful way we can purge ourselves of harmful stress and stress-related disease. In the next chapter we explore the ways in which building ourselves up physically—through exercise, proper diet, and rest—can fortify our resistance further still.

THE BOTTOM LINE

Beyond just how many or what kind of stressors we face in our lives, the distress we experience has to do with the way in which these stressors are perceived. Strengthening ourselves emotionally—through our attitude, our physical responses, and the expression of our good and bad feelings—can protect us from their impact.

Care and Feeding of the Unstressed Self

THE KEYS

• Good health habits, including routine physical exams and a sound diet, provide the foundation from which we can build a calmer, better self.

• One of the best stress relievers, exercise relaxes us physically and exorcises stress hormones.

• Relaxation techniques, from yoga to deep breathing, can calm the body and the mind.

• Things really do look better in the morning after a good night's sleep.

• True stress relief cannot be found in a bottle, but it can be achieved by leading a healthy lifestyle.

Our mental attitude has a great deal to do with what we perceive as stressful and how we cope with it. But our physical state has a lot to do with that as well. Just as anxiety can have a negative impact on our bodies, so too can our bodies affect how we deal with anxiety. By staying physically healthy—through proper diet, exercise, and getting enough rest, among other things—we won't experience as much stress and can better deal with the stresses we must face.

In earlier chapters we explored the ways in which stress can manifest itself in numerous physical symptoms, from headaches and chest pains to stomachaches and rashes and more serious problems. It can worsen ailments such as asthma and cardiac problems, turn our hair gray, and wrinkle our skin.

But it's important to remember that the opposite can be true, as well: Physiological troubles can masquerade as symptoms of stress. Those chest palpitations, in other words, might be prompted less by the rush-hour commute than by an irregularity of the heart. Your irritability might have less to do with your kids' rambunctious playmates than with the biological, age-related cycle of hormonal changes.

Physical maladies—be they colds or muscle aches or impaired vision—can also make us more susceptible to stress, lowering our emotional resistance and weakening our coping skills.

Just as it's important not to ignore the stress that might be behind a physical symptom, it's crucial not to blame a problem on stress when it might have a physiological cause. "It's up to the individual and his or her health-care provider to determine," says Donald E. Williams, Ph.D., consultant in Behavioral Medicine at the Mayo Clinic in Rochester, Minnesota. "If there are interventions that really are indicated medically, then they should be undertaken."

And there's no stress reliever like hearing your doctor say that you're well.

Migraine headaches, for instance, can be triggered by stress, but they may also be brought on by certain foods, hunger, changes in the weather, some physical activities, medications, as well as hormonal changes.

Regular checkups with health practitioners keep us up-to-date on our physical health in ways that we cannot always evaluate ourselves. And the sooner problems are detected, the less damage they can do. People at different stages of life and with varied levels of risk have different needs. Consult a physician for the right schedule of preventive care.

The Stress-Busting Merits of Exercise

Even if you don't count the stress-relieving impact of having the healthier body exercise will bring (and that counts for a lot), physical activity is without a doubt one of the best antidotes to anxiety.

Why? According to the American Council on Exercise (ACE) in San Diego, one theory is that exercise stimulates chemicals called neurotransmitters, which are produced in the brain and are believed to mediate moods and emotions. Just one exercise session, reports ACE, can generate from 90 to 120 minutes of relaxation response,

SMART MOVE

No matter how many elixirs or salves or wonder programs anyone may try to sell us, there is no magic necessary when it comes to handling stress. "Some of the popular advice that we all know and hear is good," says Donald E. Williams, Ph.D., of the Mayo Clinic in Rochester, Minnesota. "Get good exercise, try to get good rest, eat well-balanced nutrition—these are some of the best things we can do to better manage stress."

also called "postexercise euphoria" or "endorphin response," although neurotransmitters other than endorphins are involved.

In the lab, clinicians have found exercise to prompt decreases in the electrical activity of tensed muscles in people with nervous tension. These subjects were less jittery and hyperactive.

"Exercise gives us a physical outlet for the emotional stresses in our life," sums up Richard Cotton, chief exercise physiologist at ACE. "Hormones that are a byproduct of stress are meant by our very primitive physiology to be released in fight or flight, and we don't have that in our daily existence anymore—we can't physically fight someone, or run away. And that's what the exercise is: It's the physical aspect of the process that we don't otherwise have."

Without exercise, those stress hormones are left "unresolved"—elevating cholesterol levels, blood pressure, and risk of disease. With even a moderate physical workout, we can literally work the anxiety, the anger, and the stress out of our system.

Self-esteem issues also come into play. "When we're physically active, and conditioned, we tend to feel better about ourselves, and we're therefore more stress-resistant," says Cotton. "When we feel weak, tired, and lack energy, stress is that much harder to tolerate."

Aerobic exercise, such as jogging or biking, that gets the heart going is the most widely touted for stress relief, but it isn't the only kind that helps. Stretching exercises and strength or resistance training, such as weight lifting or pushups, call for more focus—counting repetitions, becoming conscious of your muscles—which takes your mind off your troubles and to a better place.

Tips

• **Start slowly.** Don't begin a rigorous exercise program all at once, especially not when you're already stressed. Increasing the physical activity in your life by even just moderate amounts—taking the stairs instead of the elevator, parking your car farther away and walking more—will make a difference.

• **Don't put more pressure on yourself than you already have by forcing yourself to exercise when you're really tired.** If you are on a regular workout schedule, be flexible during stressful times.

• **Balance your fitness program.** Incorporate aerobic activity for your heart and body composition; anaerobic activity to build muscle strength and endurance; and stretching exercises to increase your range of motion and lower your risk of injury while you're at work on the other two.

• **The best exercise is the one you will *do*.** Whether it is walking on a treadmill at a gym or taking a tour of the neighborhood, or whether it is lifting barbells or doing floor exercise, make exercise your own. Whatever you choose, do it sensibly, with a balanced, personal program that suits your needs.

• **Choose where.** If you're surrounded by people all day, a crowded gym might defeat your stress-relieving purpose, but if you're alone all day and crave the social aspect of exercising with others, a health club may be the place for you. There are plenty of options; choose the one that produces the least anxiety. And don't exercise where you work if work anxieties are what you're seeking to escape.

- **Take activity breaks during the day.** The American Council on Exercise recommends ten-minute exercise breaks every ninety minutes. You will get just as much out of these sessions as you would had you exercised for the total amount of time nonstop.

- **Play.** Tennis, racquetball, volleyball, and other active games count as exercise and can rid your body of stress-causing adrenaline and other hormones. And fun is good for you, too!

Yoga: A Different Kind of Movement

For the more than six million Americans practicing some form of it, the ancient practice of yoga is offering significant relief from the stressors of modern life.

Yoga encompasses a philosophy that goes far beyond twisting oneself into the shape of a pretzel. Beyond a set of physical positions and breathing techniques, yoga is a meditative approach and a way of life that promotes a more limber physical and mental state. Along with improved flexibility and muscle tone, yoga (like other mind-body techniques) can offer stress-reduction, improved control of bodily functions, and lowered risk of disease.

From the Sanskrit root *yuj* or *yui,* meaning to yoke, or unite, yoga combines a belief system with diet and exercise to integrate spirit, body, and mind. But you don't have to be a total convert to reap benefits. Studies have found that when large muscle groups repeatedly contract and relax, as in

Relaxing with Massage

Few would argue against the virtues of massage as one of the more pleasurable methods of stress relief. But massage therapy, or therapeutic massage, is more than just a terrific way to relax. The rubbing, kneading, pressing, and stroking offer valuable health benefits to musculoskeletal, circulatory, and nervous systems alike. The laying on of hands—an ancient approach to healing—improves the circulation that stress constricts, helps remove metabolic waste, relaxes tensed muscles, and physically distracts us from the problems of our world. The loosening of chronically stiff, aching muscles has even been credited with releasing repressed emotions hidden for years.

On-site corporate facilities to reduce stress for employees are growing in number, as are the number of massage therapists. More than thirty thousand are certified through the National Certification Board for Therapeutic Massage and Body Work, and five hundred more apply for certification each month.

Although all forms of massage involve manipulation of soft body tissues (usually with the hands, but often with the forearms, elbows, and sometimes with the feet), there are many approaches. Some of the more common include neuromuscular massage, which relies on circulation-stimulating pressure to break the stress-tension-pain cycle; shiatsu, a Japanese technique using finger pressure; and Swedish massage, the most familiar, combining long, deep, kneading strokes with movement of the joints.

You can even do it yourself.

"You won't be able to reduce chronic tension or muscular cramps, but you may be able to relieve some stress and fatigue," Elliot Greene, spokesman for the American Massage Therapy Association, told the *Detroit News*. "You can't reach all the pressure points yourself, but you might ease some discomfort."

According to Greene, although self-massage of the back would involve movements counterproductive to relaxation, other areas are easily tended to:

• **Feet:** Press your fingertips into the soles, and massage the area in small circles.

• **Arms and legs:** Systematically moving over your limbs, grasp the muscles, knead them like bread, and then release.

• **Neck:** Do backward and forward neck rolls, then from side to side. Lastly, use your fingertips to gently massage both sides of your neck.

yoga-type activities, the brain is signaled to release specific neurotransmitters that prompt feelings of relaxation and mental acuity.

Many stress-reduction techniques are based on its principles. Dean Ornish, M.D., director of the Preventive Medicine Research Institute in Sausalito, California, uses yoga along with meditation, breathing exercises, and other relaxation techniques to reverse symptoms of heart disease and encourage physical, mental, and spiritual wellness. Research confirms that stress-linked diseases respond favorably to the approach.

And you don't have to be a contortionist, either; beginner-level classes and different yoga styles can accommodate every body's level. There are several popular types of hatha yoga. Mantra yoga uses the repetition of a word or phrase to focus the mind. Pranayama yoga involves breath control. Ashtanga, also known as "power yoga," involves energetic transition from one posture to another, while iyengar yoga concentrates on precise body alignment and positioning. Gentle yoga and flow yoga are a couple of Americanized versions.

"Certainly exercise that gets the heart rate up has its benefits because that is the true resolution [of stress hormones]," says exercise physiologist Richard Cotton. "But yoga-type exercises can also be valuable because they help us to center ourselves and to slow down the mind along with a physical activity."

Food for Calmer Thought

To meet that project deadline, you're in the office at 6 A.M. Time for breakfast is out of the question, so a jumbo thermos of coffee will have to do. You skip lunch, come home late, and have a bag of chips for dinner before collapsing into bed. The next morning you wonder why you have so much trouble getting up, and why, when you do, you feel like you want to scream.

According to the American Dietary Association (ADA), the main nutritional hazard of mental duress is not that we need more nutrients because of it, but that anxiety or pressure can cause us to neglect proper dietary habits. We just don't eat as well. And the worse we eat, the worse the effects of the stress become.

"When people are under emotional stress they tend to forget that they've probably put themselves in physiological stress," says ADA spokesperson Jackie Berning, Ph.D., R.D., who is also an assistant professor of nutrition at the University of Colorado in Colorado Springs.

Not only are our bodies impacted by the surge of stress hormones—causing, among other things, food to take longer to digest and absorption of nutrients to be slowed—but our actions can compound their effects. "Under stress, some people will eat anything they can get their hands on, and others don't eat at all," says Berning.

If we stop eating, we deprive our bodies of nutrients and energy. If we overeat, we tax our systems as well as risk weight gain, which is itself a stressor. And chances are, although we may be eat-

SMART SOURCES

Center for Nutrition Policy and Promotion
1120 20th St. N.W. Suite 200, North Lobby
Washington, D.C. 20036
202-606-8000
www.usda.gov/fcs/ cnpp.htm

The USDA's Food Guide Pyramid was designed to guard against both nutritional deficiencies and excesses. At its foundation, the government's seven "Dietary Guidelines for Americans": Eat a variety of foods; get plenty of vegetables, fruits, and grains; watch for fat, saturated fat, and cholesterol; use sugars in moderation; include salt sparingly; maintain a healthy weight; and drink alcohol in moderation, if at all. For free copies of the Food Guide Pyramid and "Dietary Guidelines for Americans," write or visit this center or its Web site.

SMART MOVE

"When I'm under stress, I try to make sure that my diet is as consistent as possible and I make it a point not to skip meals," says Nadine Pazder, R.D., outpatient consultant at Morton Plant Hospital in Clearwater, Florida. "If I get hungry or my sense of resolve tends to wane, I'm going to be more likely to eat something that I know is not good for me. If I have an apple and a chocolate bar in front of me, I'll tend to go for the chocolate. As long as I'm eating on a regular schedule, and plan for a snack, it'll be something nutrient-filled."

ing too much, we're probably taking in too little of the nutrients we need.

When we're pressed for time, we're less likely to prepare proper, balanced meals or eat them in a leisurely way conducive to good digestion. When we can't sleep and become fatigued, we're more likely to turn to caffeine, sugar and other stress-response mimicking stimulants to get us through the day.

Then there are the physiological factors of the stress response, which not only affect our bodies, but what our bodies will crave. "Blood sugar balances are thrown off," says Susan Allen, R.D., L.D., C.C.N., owner of HealthWise Nutrition Consulting in Riverside, Illinois. "You'll crave a lot more sugars." Allen recommends steering away from too many sweets, which can result in mood swings and cravings for even more sweets as blood sugar levels rise and fall. Protein can help, she says, recommending a two-to-one protein-to-carbohydrate ratio. And make those complex carbohydrates, preferably of the whole-grain variety. This means starches and dietary fiber, which can be found in potatoes, enriched rice and pasta, some vegetables, and whole-grain breads and cereal. They tend to be low in calories and fat, high in fiber, and they take some time for the body to break down. In this gradual process, your blood-sugar level and energy remain fairly constant, leaving you feeling comfortably full.

"I know it sounds boring, but balance, variety, and moderation works all the time," says Anne Dubner, R.D., L.D., an American Dietetic Association spokesperson in Houston. "It's the tried-and-true answer for making your body feel better. While you're handling your stress from the neck up, balance things from the neck down. It's not a matter

Crash Diets

Concerns about being overweight can be serious stressors. In a vicious circle, overeating can lead to more stress, which can lead to yet more overeating. Worse, we can be tempted to turn to crash and fad diets.

Extreme, low-calorie diets will backfire as the body tries to protect us from ourselves. Convinced that it's starving, it slows the metabolism—our energy-burning capacity—to conserve energy. And the lowered resting metabolic rate can continue even after we resume eating normally. This explains what happens with "yo-yo dieting," where weight is gained and lost in cycles of severely restricted diets: the metabolism falls lower and lower, and weight is harder to lose each time around.

"Miracle" diets don't work either. And they, too, can be dangerous. Beware of regimes with an all-or-nothing approach that rely heavily on food supplements, or exclude major food groups—no protein, no carbohydrates, no fats.

To maximize your body's ability to burn calories, slow-and-steady weight loss of one half to one pound a week is key (note: the faster you lose weight, the more likely you'll gain it back). Cut about five hundred calories a day from your diet; eat healthy, low-fat foods; and engage in a regular exercise activity you enjoy.

of getting more of this or more of that, but getting a nice balance throughout the day."

A varied, moderate, and balanced eating plan that supplies the proper amount of nutrients and energy is essential. The body needs specific vitamins and minerals, and how we consume them, and with what foods, can help us process the nutrients better (we can absorb only so much vitamin C at a time, for instance).

The latest research is leaning away from the three square meals a day to a "grazing" approach: smaller meals, four to six times a day, give the body a more consistent supply of fuel. Also, by lessening the chance that we will be "starving" before our next meal, grazing can help us to eat more sensibly. It also allows us to be less frantic about food preparation, making meals less stressful and easier to digest.

Food and Migraine Headaches

According to the ADA, up to 20 percent of America's 23 million migraine sufferers can blame their debilitating headaches on the food they eat. Also suspect are many food additives, seasonings, and flavorings, such as monosodium glutamate (MSG), common in restaurant and processed foods like canned and dry soups, barbecue sauce, and potato chips; sodium nitrite, commonly found in hot dogs and luncheon meats; soy sauce; marinades; and meat tenderizers.

Foods and Beverages That May Trigger Migraine

Alcohol	Red wine, vermouth, champagne, and beer
Caffeine	Coffee, tea, and soft drinks
Dairy products	Aged cheeses, such as cheddar
Breads	Sourdough, fresh yeast, and homemade
Vegetables and fruits	Some types of beans (broad, Italian, lima, lentil, fava, soy), sauerkraut, peas, avocados, and overripe bananas
Snacks	Peanuts and peanut butter
Meats	Salted and cured meats (ham, corned beef, sausage, bacon, lunch meats), dried meats, pickled herring, and chicken livers
Soups	Canned or from mixes
Desserts	Chocolate based

Source: American Dietary Association

Tips

• **Don't binge.** Don't eat the first thing you see when you open the refrigerator door. If you feel as though you're "starving," grab a healthful snack such as some crisp, raw veggies, plain yogurt, or fruit, to sustain you until you can prepare a well-balanced meal.

• **Don't pressure yourself to prepare a gourmet meal from scratch.** If you're pressed for time, take advantage of the growing number of prepared salads and heat-and-serve entrées in the supermarket, or order in.

• **Avoid fast-food meals.** These are usually laden more with fats and calories than nutrients. Skip these to help the body come out of the stress response healthier and feeling better.

• **Start your morning with a healthful breakfast.** Doing this will energize you for the day ahead.

• **Handle high-fiber foods with care.** If you are anticipating a stressful event, say, for example, a public-speaking engagement in the morning, stay away from high-fiber foods that can throw your gastrointestinal system into turmoil. To be sure you're not running on empty, eat especially well the night before, avoiding heavy spices.

• **Avoid sugars.** This includes the lactose in milk products and the fructose in fruits. These simple carbohydrates are absorbed quickly by the body and cause blood-sugar levels to leap, and then drop, which can leave you feeling drained and hungry again.

F.Y.I.

More than 100 million Americans of all ages regularly fail to get a good night's sleep.

At least eighty-four types of disorders of sleeping and waking interfere with quality of life and personal health.

Source: American Sleep Disorders Association

Get a Good Night's Sleep

Like other basics, getting enough rest is key to keeping ourselves healthy. And the healthier we are, the less susceptible we are to the stressors we encounter while we're awake.

Lack of sleep, on the other hand, lowers our immunity and makes us more susceptible to physical illness, itself a stressor, which in turn can leave us vulnerable to other stressors we face. Increased irritability, clouded thinking, and physical weakness wreak havoc upon our coping skills. We're less able to focus, we make more mistakes, we forget what we need to remember, and we are more likely to react with our emotions than with our heads.

"Good health requires good sleep," Quentin Regestein, M.D., states simply in *Sleep Problems and Solutions.*

"If our bodies do not get enough sleep, many disease processes can be aggravated, from conditions related to the autoimmune and central nervous systems to arthritis and other pain problems to psychological disorders," says Regestein, director of the sleep clinic at Boston's Brigham and Women's Hospital and a professor at Harvard Medical School. "Even mild sleep loss can reduce our ability to think clearly and slow our reaction time."

But the amount of sleep we need per night varies so much from person to person and at different stages of our lives that putting a number on how many hours we should get could keep anyone tossing and turning all night long.

"The only way to tell whether you've had enough is how you function during the day on a sustained basis," says Peter Hauri, Ph.D., of the Sleep Disorders Center at Mayo Clinic Rochester, in Minnesota. "If you are not sleepy when you watch TV at night or are sitting in a boring meeting, then you probably had enough."

"The evidence would show that in the United States now, we are likely to sleep deprive ourselves voluntarily," Hauri adds. "Ever since Edison invented the light bulb, we've cut down one and a half hours per night." And according to the American Sleep Disorders Association (ASDA) in Rochester, Minnesota, more than 100 million Americans of all ages regularly fail to manage a good night's worth.

But while rest is more important than ever to the stressed body, operating, as it is, at high gear for sustained periods of time, there's the obvious quandary: The more stressed we are, and the more we need sleep, the more trouble we have falling asleep, and the sleep we get when we do may be more troubled. Several bedtime routines can help.

Tips

• **Don't eat a heavy meal before bedtime.**

• **Cut back on caffeine, alcohol, and tobacco consumption, especially with or after dinner.** This includes soft drinks and chocolate. Have herbal teas instead, such as chamomile or valerian, both of which are known relaxants.

• **Keep a regular sleep schedule.** To keep your internal sleep clock running on time, try to get out of bed at the same time every morning, including

SMART SOURCES

American Sleep
  Disorders
  Association
6301 Bandel Road
Suite 101
Rochester, MN 55901
www.asda.org

This professional medical association offers a wide range of helpful wellness booklets on sleep and sleep disorders, from Circadian rhythms (the body's natural sleep/wake cycle) to snoring. For a list of available booklets, visit the ASDA web site or write to the organization, enclosing a self-addressed, stamped envelope. A referral list of accredited sleep disorders centers in your area is also available.

How Do You Usually Sleep?

On your side 59%

On your back 18%

On your stomach 13%

Other 4%

Don't know/no response 6%

Source: Bruskin-Goldring Research

weekends. Keeping steady, regular times for eating meals, taking medications, doing chores, and other activities can also help.

• **Establish a presleep ritual.** Activities such as a warm bath and fifteen minutes of a soothing book (that means no suspense thrillers) each night will start you off to a good night's sleep. Remember: the purpose is to wind down.

• **Do not nap to "catch up."** The proper balance of mental and physical activity throughout the day will help you to sleep better at sleeping time. If you do take regular naps, try to do so at the same time every day.

• **Make your bedroom a stress-free zone.** You should associate your bedroom with peace, rest, and loving intimacy with your partner. Keep out all tension-producing objects and tasks (like office work and required reading); shades down; and the television off.

• **Invest in a quality mattress and bedding.**

• **Don't force yourself to slumber.** Go to bed only when you are sleepy.

• **Exercise regularly.** A study reported in the *Journal of the American Medical Association* found that subjects with sleep disorders who participated in a moderate exercise program enjoyed a better overall quality of sleep, fell asleep faster, and managed to sleep longer than those who didn't exercise. But if you do exercise, don't do so close to your bedtime. The ASDA recommends at least six hours beforehand for those who exercise vigorously; at least four hours for mild exercisers.

• **Avoid sleeping pills, or use them conservatively.** And never use medications while having alcohol.

Don't Wait to Exhale . . . or Inhale

The expression "as natural as breathing" may not serve us as well as it sounds. The truth is, the way most of us tend to breathe naturally isn't sufficient to provide our bodies with the oxygen we need during times of stress.

To compensate for the physical changes that occur during the stress response—when we tend to breathe more quickly and more shallowly—calls for even deeper breaths than we normally take. Instead, we tend to go in the opposite direction, often holding our breath entirely through tense moments. Ever notice the sigh that often follows a stressful moment? Take it as your body's way of saying, "I've let it out, now let a whole lot back in."

When we're tense or panicking we breathe from our chest, using more muscles and more energy to draw shallower breaths than when we use "diaphragmatic" or "deep" breathing—breathing from "the gut," with muscles below the lungs. An easy way to tell is to simply watch what's moving when you're breathing: Is it your chest or your stomach going up and down?

SMART DEFINITION

Insomnia

The National Institutes of Health defines insomnia not by the number of hours of sleep you get or how long it takes you to fall asleep, but as the perception or complaint of inadequate or poor-quality sleep because of one or more of the following: difficulty falling asleep; waking up frequently during the night with difficulty returning to sleep; waking up too early in the morning; unrefreshing sleep.

Diaphragmatic breathing slows and calms us in many ways. It can lower our heart rate and blood pressure, relax muscles, and clear our minds. Not only will deep breathing supply the body with more oxygen but it will do so with less effort.

One of the chief benefits of deep breathing is that you can do it anywhere—waiting in line at the bank, at a staff meeting, while listening to someone you don't want to hear. And it's one of the easiest, quickest relaxation techniques there is.

Ed T. Prothro, of the Association of Christian Meditators, uses the words "so hum" as a "breathing mantra" for stress reduction. "The 'so' tends to open the nose and throat wider on inhalation," according to Prothro, "and 'hum' completes the diaphragmatic breathing, a process known to reduce stress."

Without saying the words aloud, inhale while thinking "so" and exhale while thinking "hum." And if you'd like to test its effectiveness, reverse the two and see how much differently your respiration feels.

The United States Olympic Committee recommends the deep breathing exercise on the following page as a relaxation exercise for athletes to learn better control of body and mind. "With continued practice of this exercise, you will be able to relax yourself 'on the spot'—before and during competition when you are tense or anxious and have only a few moments to get your mind and body under control."

Breathing Exercise

We don't need to be participating in an Olympic event to benefit from the breathing method described below by the U.S. Olympic Committee.

• Get physically comfortable, uncross your arms and legs and close your eyes.

• Take a moment to clear your mind of any distracting thoughts or images.

• Become aware of how you are breathing. Is it fast? Slow? Rhythmic? Put a hand on your stomach—feel your stomach rising and falling with each breath.

• Now, take a deep breath—feel your diaphragm expanding—and hold it for two seconds. As you slowly exhale, say to yourself, "Relaaax." Take another deep breath and again hold it for two seconds. This time, as you slowly exhale, say to yourself, "Relaxed and ready."

• Repeat this again, making sure your mind is clear of any distracting thoughts.

• Take a deep breath from your diaphragm, hold it two seconds, and exhale while slowly saying, "Relaaax" to yourself.

• When you are ready, take another deep breath from your diaphragm, hold it, and exhale while saying to yourself, "Relaxed and ready."

Source: United States Olympic Committee

False Serenity

Misguided attempts to cope with stress have led many to abuse substances like alcohol, nicotine, and marijuana—none of which will help and all of which present potential harm.

Many medications are now available, including antidepressants and sedatives or hypnotics for sleep; and anxiolytics or tranquilizers for panic attacks.

Those with severe anxiety disorders who cannot find relief through stress management techniques may benefit from appropriate medications prescribed by their physicians. The risk of dependency on nonprescribed substances, however, may merit some anxious thought.

Many over-the-counter preparations promise to help, not the least of which are vitamin and mineral products—thirty-four hundred of them, on which we spend $4 billion a year, according to the American Dietary Association. Like elixirs and tonics of old, a growing array of wonders beckons from health-store shelves. Concoctions with names such as "Slumber" contain "bio-chelated herbal extracts" of ingredients such as passion flowers and valerian root.

Can we believe the promises?

"As long as they do not claim to diagnose, treat, cure, or prevent a specific disease," says the Food and Drug Administration, "dietary supplements can claim a wide range of feel-good effects."

There are certain dangers, though. Dietary supplements—including vitamins, minerals, herbs, botanicals, and animal products—are not required to prove their safety or effectiveness. Also, megadoses of single-nutrient supplements can lead to harmful levels of some vitamins and minerals or block the effects of others you need. And with no requirement to prove exactly which parts of an herb are actually in the product—certain portions of some herbs are hazardous to health—the door is left open for fraud and health risks.

Then there's the issue of absorption: many vitamins contain more of a substance than the body can process at a time. The result is what Victor Herbert, M.D., coauthor of *The Vitamin Pushers,* calls "expensive urine."

Many people substitute supplements for nutrition. However, as ADA spokesperson Jackie Berning explains: "There are no calories associated with food supplements, so [a person taking supplements instead of following a balanced diet will] have no energy to face the next day, and that makes the stress even worse."

Beyond the basic care and feeding of the body, numerous other techniques are preferable to the pharmaceutical course. In the next chapter, we explore several.

THE BOTTOM LINE

With a solid foundation of good nutrition, physical activity, adequate rest, and good health habits, we can face day-to-day anxieties with serene strength. Feed your body properly and you'll have more energy to exercise; live an active lifestyle and you'll sleep better; get better rest and you'll be better able to cope with mental stress; feel relaxed and your body will process nutrients better. It all works together, for you.

Breaking the Cycle of Stress

No matter what we do to prevent or fortify ourselves against it, stress is an unavoidable part of life. If we let it continue unabated, we become more susceptible to other stressors down the line, and a downward spiral of anxiety ensues. It doesn't have to. By turning our minds in a more positive direction—one of joy and calm and peace—we can break the cycle.

Music Can Calm the Most Savage Stress

Just as a rousing march can summon patriotic fervor, love songs can conjure a romantic mood, and striking up the band can enliven a party, the right types of music can have a powerful effect on anxiety levels.

"Sound creates a vibration that impacts both our nervous system and the more subtle realms of body and mind," says psychologist Ronald L. Mann, Ph.D., author of *Sacred Healing: Integrating Spirituality with Psychotherapy.* "And there's a science about which notes and chords affect us in different ways."

Only in our own culture could this be considered revolutionary thinking. Indian "ragas" have long included compositions for morning, afternoon, and evening; for stimulating the nervous system, and for slowing it down. In the classical Chinese approach to medicine, music has played an important role for thousands of years.

"Certain musical compositions in various keys with certain ranges of notes will create a harmonic that affects our consciousness," says Mann. "It can shift what goes on in our physical bodies, where stress is usually held. And just the opposite is true as well—certain music is pretty toxic."

Many of us have used music's powers intuitively when we've gravitated toward sad songs to work through feelings of a broken heart, or unrequited love. When we're ready to move on to healing, we head toward livelier, more optimistic tunes.

Music therapy—both listening and making melody—has been helping people at every stage of life, with everything from Alzheimer's disease to substance abuse to rehabilitation from physical injury and pain. In hospitals, psychiatric facilities, nursing homes, schools, even prisons, it's been used to help elevate mood, counteract depression, relax and sedate, induce sleep, calm fears, and reduce muscle tension. "A substantial body of literature exists to support the effectiveness of music therapy," according to the American Music Therapy Association (AMTA).

Although the theory that music can soothe the savage breast is not at all a new one, music therapy found its roots as a profession following World Wars I and II, when the physical and emotional response of hospitalized veterans was bettered by visits from community musicians. The first music therapy degree program was offered at Michigan State University in 1944.

"Healthy individuals can use music for stress reduction via active music-making, such as drumming, as well as passive listening for relaxation," says AMTA, which also notes that music can play an important supportive role in exercise, a major stress reliever.

California-based concert pianist and composer Shirley E. Kaiser, M.A., has a special interest in harmonies' healing powers.

"The notes of A and B below middle C affect your heart in a very healing way," says Kaiser, whose CD, *Journey Within,* features meditative instrumentals. Volume, notes, chords, rhythm, harmony, and tempo all have an impact. Just think of the soundtrack of *Jaws,* and how it makes you feel; then think of the *Love Story* theme.

Tips

• **Go slow, and avoid dissonant or clashing harmonies and sounds.** Music that is melodious and corresponds with a slow, relaxed heart rate will cause your body to respond in like manner. Blood pressure and heart rate will lower.

• **Listen to what you like.** From classical to rap to jazz formats, you can find rhythms to soothe the spirit and ease the soul. Listen to the music and to how your body responds.

"People know what's soothing," says psychologist Ronald Mann. "Basically if what you're listening to leaves you peaceful, soothed, inspired, joyful, filled with love—those are the compositions that will bring peace of mind and well-being."

• **Choose instrumentals over songs with lyrics.** If you're trying to clear your mind, words might be distracting. At other times, singing along might provide release.

• **Stay in the here and now.** Musical journeys down memory lane won't always take you to a better place. Songs that you associate with painful remembrances can bring up old anxieties.

• **Give it time.** A study on the effects of music on physiological responses (using classical music) reported in the *Journal of Music Therapy* found that the sedative effect of music was more apparent in the second half of the pieces.

• **Try Mother Nature's greatest hits.** Recordings of natural environmental sounds—the ocean, waterfalls, the rustle of leaves in the wind—allow us to tune out modern-day noise pollution and all the stressors that go with it.

Visual Effects

What we hear, what we see, even what we imagine we've seen and heard, all manifest themselves in various ways within our minds, and so within our bodies. The disturbing image of a violent car accident can remain with us for days, weeks, or even longer, affecting our stress levels, our sleep patterns, and our appetites. The good news is that health-affirming, stress-relieving, calming images can have a lasting effect as well.

What You See and How You Stress

When they noticed that viewers of an art and technology project incorporating symmetrical kaleidoscopic images from nature always came away "blissfully drowsy," Nancy and Paul Miller of Kaleidoscope Arts took note. "Not good for art," they thought, "but very good for body and mind."

Nancy, who worked in advertising, which she compares to "jumping in the Cuisinart every day," was herself "beyond jangled," yet reported that "the constantly changing kaleidoscopic images moving before my eyes to this restful rhythm had this amazing calming-down effect."

When the Millers learned that two hospitals were using their images for stress management, they created their video *Journey: A Kaleidoscopic Trip to Inner Peace*, an excursion into nature with a score incorporating bird calls, wind chimes, and waterfalls into symphonic bliss.

With so much medical proof of the positive effects of nature, music, and imagery on everything from blood pressure to immune system response, it's no surprise that clinics and hospitals nationwide are using *Journey* and other imagery tapes to help their patients.

But images don't have to be in motion to relax us. Mandalas, from the Sanskrit for circle, are complex circular designs, intended to draw the eye inward to the center and are used for contemplative focus by many meditators and others. No wonder why there are so many peaceful landscapes and still lifes adorning therapists' walls.

Like music, both the creation and observation of art can change us, affecting our autonomic nervous system, our hormone levels, our blood flow, and our emotional state.

Tips

• **Turn off the TV.** It is mesmerizing, but chances are the images on the television screen will do nothing but raise your stress levels. You'd do better to turn it off and watch the empty screen.

• **Look around you.** "Live" images add an extra component to the relaxation response. Try gazing out at the ocean to the sound of crashing waves, as your bare toes dig into the sand; or look into a blazing fireplace, with the crackle of flames and the fragrance of aromatic firewood in the air.

In the Mind's Eye

Images don't have to be physical to be effective—one of the most popular stress management techniques involves imagined scenes.

Organizations as mainstream as the U.S. Olympic Committee encourage the use of mental imagery—or visualization—for athletes to relax and focus prior to an event. It even offers a suggested "Go to the Beach" exercise to take yourself away from stress and anxiety.

A study published in *Health Psychology* on the effects of guided imagery and music (GIM) therapy on mood and cortisol in healthy adults found that after six biweekly sessions, the participants reported significant decreases in depression, fatigue, and cortisol level, related to decreases in mood disturbances. The authors conclude that even a short trial of GIM may help healthy adults.

"The use of imagination is very powerful," says psychologist Ronald Mann, who cites studies in which physical therapists would ask subjects to visualize the use of a muscle without actually moving it and would find the body responding in "very minute but tangible ways to just one's state of mind."

"The nature of energy is that it follows thought," says Mann. "So if you concentrate and in

SMART DEFINITION

Progressive relaxation

A combination of imagery and physical release that helps you relax. By tensing individual muscles or muscle groups for about ten seconds at a time and then loosening, then tensing and loosening again and again, you'll feel the body untightening, unwinding from pent-up stress. Guided imagery tapes can be helpful, leading you to relax literally from head to toe.

SMART DEFINITION

Frequency-following effect

The tendency of our brainwave activity to "follow" flickering light and pulsating rhythms, particularly in the frequencies associated with relaxation. It is one of the reasons why we find gazing into a fire or listening to certain rhythms so calming. Combining pulsing light with certain musical beats can be particularly effective.

your mind create a particular image that is healthy and healing, it starts a different kind of flow of energy into your body."

Your visualization doesn't have to be anatomically correct, either; you needn't know where your stress hormones are coming from or where they'll go. Bathing yourself in light, for instance, and feeling it calm you with warmth and comfort can have a healing result.

Tips

• **Keep it quiet.** Although you can use imagery techniques most any time and place, the best way to practice in the beginning is within a quiet, peaceful environment. A number of guided imagery tapes are available to help you learn how.

• **Try "traveling."** Take yourself to a place that brings you solace. Is it the beach? A meadow? The fireplace of a quaint cottage in the woods? Ticket prices or lack of accommodations can't hold you back.

• **Include all the senses.** See a scene in detail, smell the flowers in the meadow, hear the chirping of birds, feel the breeze on your face, taste a blade of grass in your mouth, and feel your body unwind. The more vivid and real the experience, the better.

• **Use a stop sign.** If intrusive thoughts float into your consciousness, picture a red light or a stop sign, then give a the green light to the images you chose.

Friends and Family: The Social Safety Net

When the baby is crying, you have a doctor's appointment, the car won't start, and your membership with AAA just expired, the words of a friend saying, "Don't worry. I'll watch little Louie, and here are the keys to my car," are worth a thousand times their weight in tranquilizers.

When things seem out of control, having someone to whom we can turn is comforting not only in terms of the practical help he can often provide but in the mere knowledge that he is there by your side.

Of course, no matter how well-meaning, our neighbors or family members will not be able to whisk away the rush-hour traffic through which we have to drive on our commute to the office, but sometimes they can suggest an alternate route, or a relaxing CD to listen to during the ride. Beyond that, having a shoulder to cry on or an ear to bend during hard times is more valuable in the long run than any particular piece of advice or physical assistance. The health benefits our intimates provide us by allowing us to express—and exorcise—our anxieties has been proven time and again, from strengthening our immune systems to bettering the health of our heart, as we've learned in earlier chapters.

There are two basic theories of social support. One—sometimes referred to as the "buffering" hypothesis—is that the presence of another when we're under acute stress can diminish the stress response then and there. The second view posits that the long-term presence of someone in our lives provides an ongoing feeling of security from which we can draw strength. There's little question that both apply.

Tips

• **Don't rule out people who aren't relatives.** If you don't have family living nearby, or simply aren't emotionally close with your relatives, special friends and neighbors can be the sister and brother you wish you had. Coworkers and classmates, fellow club and team members, or those with whom you share common interests on volunteer committees or community boards are just some of the people who can help.

• **Be human.** Social support is only as helpful as we allow it to be. Don't allow the need to look perfect keep you from sharing your humanity.

A Human's Best Friend

More than mere fetchers of paper and slippers, more than soft balls of fur that enjoy playing with string and catnip, pets can be very effective relievers of anxiety.

Many of the same theories of social support that apply to human companionship are relevant to animal companionship as well. Animal companions can serve both as a buffer during particular events and as emotion-stabilizers because of their long-term presence. In a series of studies on pets' ability to calm their owners, Karen M. Allen, Ph.D., a research scientist at the State University of New York at Buffalo School of Medicine, subjected married couples, the elderly, and women and their best friends to psychological stressors, such as public speaking, and to stressors of a physical nature, such as immersing subjects' hands in cold water. She also looked at pets' impact on life under ordinary circumstances. In every case, the presence of a pet produced lower blood pressure levels and heart rates than those that occurred when the subject was accompanied by another human being or was on his or her own.

It turns out that not even husbands and wives can compete with pets when it comes to stress reduction. Among the married couples studied, stress response was highest with spouses present and lowest with only pets, when heartbeats averaged thirty beats per minute slower. "If you must have a spouse," hypothesizes Allen, "maybe you ought to have a dog, too."

Four-legged, winged, finned, or with scales, other types of pets would likely have a similar effect, says Allen, who emphasizes that what counts is the bond between man (or woman) and beast. The unconditional love they offer is reassuring. "We perceive pets to be nonevaluative," says Allen. "They may be laughing at us, but we don't think they are." And they never violate our confidentiality.

"Pets help people face situations in a calmer way," according to the Delta Society in Renton, Washington, a nonprofit organization dedicated to promoting public awareness of the positive effects of animals on health and human development. "We tend to speak more slowly and softly to our pet than we do with other people." They teach us to act—and be—more relaxed.

STREET SMARTS

"During a thunderstorm, eighteen-year-old, five-foot-five me was cowering in my room, while little two-pound Elvis the chihuahua was oblivious," says Cara Naiditch, a student in Pasadena, California. "He is such a strong little guy! And comforting. I figure that if he isn't worried, then I should be okay."

Forty-four-year-old Chris Mackay in New Bedford, Massachusetts, adds, "The only thing that brings down my stress level is my dogs. They seem to calm me down just by sitting on my lap or licking me. They love me for me, imperfections and all. All I have to do is look in those big brown eyes and everything gets just a little better."

SMART SOURCES

Delta Society
289 Perimeter Road E.
Renton, WA 98055
800-869-6898
http://petsforum.com/
deltasociety/
default.html

In addition to supporting research, this nonprofit clearinghouse for information on human-animal interactions and animal-assisted therapy offers a Pet Partners program that trains volunteers and screens their pets—from dogs and cats to potbellied pigs and parrots—for visiting hospitals, nursing homes, rehabilitation centers, and schools. Almost two thousand "teams" throughout the country reap the combined stress-relieving benefits of animal interaction and helping others.

The relaxation response that comes from touching or cuddling an animal; the healthy exercise they prompt us to undertake; the security they provide on lonely evenings; the laughter they give us along the way—these are just some of the many benefits research has confirmed.

And then there are the social benefits.

"She can turn an elevator of strangers into a group of smiling, chatting, 'old friends' in less than six floors," writes Susan Chernak McElroy, coauthor with Michael W. Fox of *Animals as Teachers and Healers: True Stories and Reflections,* of her dog's impact on strangers. "Any room she graces becomes an instant mecca of goodwill, happy faces, and workers rolling around on the floor for a therapeutic dog kiss and hug."

Tips

• **You don't have to own a pet to benefit.** "Interacting with a friendly but unfamiliar dog can help reduce consequences of stress," according to the Delta Society, as can watching tropical fish in a tank at the doctor's office.

• **You do have to care.** "A positive attitude toward the animal is necessary for the animal to decrease stress levels," say the experts at Delta. Karen Allen's research subjects proved the point: "If they treated a cat like a pillow," she says, "they got the emotional support of a pillow." Do not get a pet solely for the purpose of anxiety reduction—these are sentient, living creatures who need love and caretaking and not an owner who will view them as only tools.

Doing Good Works

There's another form of social involvement that not only lowers our stress levels but, in the process, makes the world a better place: volunteering.

Helping those in need—be they the homeless, the disabled, or even the always-impoverished non-profit arts groups—brings us into the company of others of like mind, with all the stress-reducing elements that includes. While we're at it, our minds are off our own problems, and our self-esteem grows.

When writer Allan Luks asked magazine readers to share their experiences with volunteering, many reported "rushes of physical pleasure and well-being, increased energy, warmth, and actual relief from aches and pains." Findings from a larger survey led him to write *The Healing Power of Doing Good: The Health and Spiritual Benefits of Helping Others.*

"What I call the helper's high," writes Luks, "involves physical sensations that strongly indicate a sharp reduction in stress, and the release of the body's natural painkillers, the endorphins. This initial rush is then followed by a longer-lasting period of improved emotional well-being. In effect, helping produces within the helper a two-part response—the healthy helping syndrome. Exercise and good nutrition alone, for all their power to keep us healthy, are not enough."

"It is not necessary to wait until you have an opportunity to donate a kidney or save the whole world to enjoy the good feeling of calm and human kinship," Luks continues. "A small effort to help one person can create these same feelings and attitudes, emotions that, if they occur regularly in our

SMART SOURCES

VolunteerAmerica!
P.O. Box 1788
Blairsden, CA 96103
530-836-0707
www.volunteer-
america.com

VolunteerAmerica!
helps individuals,
families, groups, and
organizations find
volunteer opportunities
at national parks coun-
trywide—from leading
environmental tours or
photographing wildlife
to designing computer
programs and helping
with brochures.

stressful world, can lead to better physical health, better mental health, and overall happiness."

Other studies indicate that face-to-face helping is best. "The more contact with others, the better for us," write Robert E. Ornstein, Ph.D., and David S. Sobel, M.D., in *Healthy Pleasures*. "We need to meet the people we help, see their lives, connect with them."

Tips

• **Take it easy.** Start out by giving one or two hours at a time. Cramming your good works into an already cramped schedule can swiftly turn a pleasure into another obligatory pain.

• **Enlist a friend to participate.** Not only can the companionship help you get started if you're hesitant, but the volunteer organization will gain from another pair of hands.

• **Don't compare your contribution with another's.** What matters is that you're both giving of yourselves, not competing.

• **Do what you like.** Thousands of opportunities exist, covering every area of interest, skill, and location. Local volunteer bureaus can help steer you to the right place.

• **Try a little kindness every day.** Perform a random act, and bask in the pleasure.

Have Fun

Once upon a time in our lives—before appointment calendars, alarm-clock wristwatches, teleconferenced meetings, and "doing lunch"—we had "play days." We didn't make appointments. We didn't pencil each other in. There was no particular time-slot for Mr. Potato Head or Monopoly; no carefully budgeted calendar squares for marbles, hopscotch, or hide-and-seek.

It was all just play time. Spontaneous enjoyment of all of the activities of our choice. And then time passed. We grew up. We got calendars. And the fun seemed to get scheduled out of our adult lives . . . right around the time the tension headaches, and ulcers began.

The concept of scheduling fun may be difficult to swallow, but if we don't, grown-up life tends to steal it away. Make time for the kid in you—time for what you want, not have, to do—and some of that stress-free enjoyment will return.

The calendar entry can read "movies with Nancy" or "Matisse exhibit with Bruce"; "crafts fair" or "picnic lunch." The activity matters less than the time put aside. Some of the best times, in fact, are those simply marked "play," leaving the time—and you—open to possibility.

Tips

• **Play indoors.** Spend an afternoon looking at old photographs, boxes of correspondence, or schoolday memories. Perish the thought of any filing, labeling, or organizing; no work allowed.

• **Play outdoors.** Try setting out without either your agenda or wristwatch. Play "tourist" and let a guide lead you among local points of interest you never really looked at before, letting you in on the history and secrets of your own hometown.

• **Play alone.** Move at your own pace, try and indulge your own curiosity in your own way without looking over your shoulder to gauge a companion's attention span. In the privacy of your playtime you can sketch the world as you see it, or play a favorite musical piece and "conduct" the Philharmonic with a baton of a wooden-spoon.

• **Play with others.** Sharing an experience can multiply the joy. "Look at this!" "What in the world is that?" Shared memories enrich friendships and draw people closer. Create "remember whens." And you don't have to confine yourself to human playmates (see "A Human's Best Friend," on page 156).

Pamper Yourself

Long, hot baths have been time-honored prescriptions for stress relief. Before we knew anything about the scientific benefits of heat and water on our circulatory or musculoskeletal systems, we knew that they worked.

A luxurious soak in a warm tub causes blood vessels to relax and dilate, lowering blood pressure, muscle tension, and anxiety level. Immersed in water, we're more buoyant; neither our troubles nor gravity weigh us down as much. If we're fortunate enough to have a Jacuzzi or hot tub, the swirling, massaging action can provide a form of

Sex: Good for You

Hormones and endorphins triggered by lovemaking cause the entire body to relax. The problem: when you're stressed, having sex may well be the last thing on your mind. The good news is that many of the relaxation techniques associated with stress relief can reinvigorate the libido as well.

• Turn off the phone, dim the lights, put on some stress-relieving music, and put all distractions out of sight and mind.

• Start with relaxing massage or touch. Don't even think about where things may lead you. Lie down, close your eyes, and let your partner explore your body. Or vice versa. Let events go where they will, or not.

• Don't be "goal oriented." Enjoy the process. Whether or not you reach intercourse or orgasm, caressing and touch are not only pleasurable but will work wonders for your mental and physical health.

• You *can* go it alone For some physical pleasures, partners are very nice, but not necessary. And we promise you won't go blind.

hydrotherapy, which some studies have linked with the release of endorphins, our bodies' naturally produced pain-killers.

Add a few easily accessible ingredients to that tub, and the recipe for tranquillity becomes even more effective. There's more to a bubble bath, in other words, than froth.

"Perception of odors can have a major impact on memory, learning, emotions, thinking, and feeling," according to the Atlantic Institute of Aromatherapy (AIA) in Tampa, Florida. Beyond the sensory pleasure of pleasant fragrances, aromatherapy uses essential oils—highly concentrated extracts of flowers, herbs, grasses, shrubs, trees, and plants—to enhance our state of well-being, both physically and mentally.

F.Y.I.

Essential Oils Helpful for Stress Relief:

Chamomile

Geranium

Jasmine

Lavender

Marjoram

Rose

Ylang Ylang

Source: Cheryl Hoard, National Association for Holistic Aromatherapy, as quoted by FitnessLink Web site

When used by masseurs, the application of these oils to the skin can dilate the blood vessels, which, in turn, causes warming of underlying muscles, according to AIA. "In addition, because of the effect of relaxation on the brain and the subsequent sedating or stimulating of the nervous system, essential oils can also indirectly raise and lower blood pressure."

Inhaling the oils can also have an effect. "Because of olfaction's direct connection to the brain," AIA continues, "sending electrical messages directly into the limbic system, essential oils can have effects on emotions and mental states."

As therapeutic agents, essential oils work similarly to tranquilizers. Specific scents, such as lavender, are calming and sedative. Used improperly, however, or at full strength, they can be as dangerous as any drug. Find out what you're doing, first.

Tips

• **Add to the experience.** Bring some beautiful artwork or hanging plants into your bathing area. Add some relaxing music, candlelight, and calm, deep breaths.

• **Take the phone off the hook.** You know it's a law of nature that a call will come in as soon as you're immersed. Don't let it happen.

• **Don't let the pampering stop at your bathroom door.** Bringing art, fresh flowers, and beauty into every area of your life, and taking "news fasts" to leave some of the ugliness out, are among the life-enhancement strategies advocated by popular health guru Andrew Weil, M.D. Indulge in a salon

Jet Lag

Jet lag not only leaves us craving dinner at bedtime and sleep at dawn but wreaks havoc on numerous body cycles.

• Several days before departure, start to change your eating and sleeping schedule. If you're headed west, go to bed an hour later each day, and sleep later in the morning. If you're flying east, go to bed and wake up earlier. In either case, get plenty of rest.

• If you're crossing just one or two time zones for only a brief stay, keep your watch—and your schedule—on home time.

• Schedule your flight to arrive as close to your regular bedtime as possible. Then go to bed, and try to sleep until a sensible hour.

• Don't nap; it will only prolong the adaptation process.

• Get out in the sun. Exposure to daylight helps reset your body clock.

treatment—complete with massage and manicure. You know what they say about how you feel when you look good . . .

Have a Great Vacation

Getting away from it all—literally—can provide welcome relief from the trials and tribulations of day-to-day life. While away, it can be that much easier to let go of the cares of keeping house, advancing our careers, and watching the clock. Time away allows us time for renewal, revival, refreshment, and replenishment of our souls.

For some, a luxury retreat is most calming, with hotel staff at the ready, waiters at one's beck and

WHAT MATTERS, WHAT DOESN'T

What Matters

• Relaxing to music you enjoy.

• Visualizing yourself in a beautiful place.

• Being able to turn to a family member or friend for emotional support.

• Setting aside time to pamper yourself.

• A vacation that truly takes you away from your cares.

What Doesn't

• Ravi Shankar.

• Whether the beautiful place you're visualizing is real.

• That your brother or sister is, technically, a neighbor or friend.

• Setting yourself aside to pamper everyone else.

• Do-everything, be-everywhere tours.

call, concierges arranging day trips, in-room massages on demand. For others, a week of solid physical activity brings solace by way of walking tours of exotic locations; water sports; volunteer work on an archeological dig. Or perhaps a remote lakeside cabin is your answer to escape, far from everyone and everything; no sound but nature and your own voice.

What were once considered esoteric vacation "alternatives" have now become mainstream; even travel expert Arthur Frommer touts yoga-based resorts. Some travel agencies, such as Resort2Fitness, specialize in "vacations for the mind, body, and spirit," from the austerity of a Buddhist ashram to ultraluxe accommodations to the tune of $4,000-plus per week.

Whatever your preference, what's most important is exactly that: that it is your preference. The point is to enjoy yourself, not to relocate your tensions to an out-of-town locale.

Avoid pretrip anxieties by visiting a local travel agency, where professionals can guide you through what can be an overwhelming world of possibilities and help you obtain everything from visas to show tickets. (Look for the initials CTC, for Certified Travel Counselor, after your agent's name.)

Exploring vacation sites on the Internet is another option (six million travelers booked trips online in 1997), but beware. "In an age where there is so much information on the Internet, we're finding that a lot of people are suffering from information overload," says Steve Loucks, of the American Society of Travel Agents in Alexandria, Virginia. "Clients are coming in armed with so many more facts, but those facts can be contradictory with what's actually available out there."

Tips

• **Destination known.** If you're traveling with companions, get them involved in the selection of your destination from the start to avoid the stress of bearing all that decision-making on your own.

• **Don't try to do everything.** As in your "real" life, unrealistic expectations of what you can do within a given time frame will backfire. Expecting to find relaxation, activity, total familiarity with a foreign country, *and* instant revival will stress you out of the possibility that any of the above will occur.

• **Make a change.** If you live in the city, visit the country, and vice versa. Especially if you travel a lot on business, the optimal escape should be far from where you usually go for work and leave no question that you're on vacation.

• **Get out of touch.** Unless absolutely necessary, leave the cell phone, fax machine, e-mail, beeper, and pager at home.

• **Get out.** Communing with nature is an integral part of our well-being, so wherever you are, spend as much time as possible outdoors.

Of course, the ultimate goal is not to have to travel far away in search of escape from our stressors, but to find serenity within. By reducing the number of anxiety producers around us, minimizing the negative effect they have on our lives, fortifying ourselves with healthy bodies, and keeping a mental attitude that takes things in stride, we can find that peace.

THE BOTTOM LINE

Music and art; companionship and enjoyment; sights, smells, and experiences that bring us joy are some of the most important tools we have for coping with anxiety. The more pleasure, the more beauty, the more delights we find in living, the less room we leave open to be occupied by negative feelings. Stress may be an inevitable part of existence, but it does not have to define our lives.

Index

Books in the Smart Guide™ Series

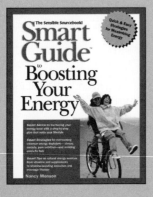

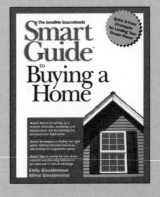

Smart Guide™ to
Boosting Your Energy

Smart Guide™ to
Buying a Home

Smart Guide™ to
Getting Strong and Fit

Smart Guide™ to
Getting Thin and
Healthy

Smart Guide™ to
Healing Foods

Smart Guide™ to
Making Wise
Investments

Smart Guide™ to
Managing Personal
Finance

Smart Guide™ to
Managing Your Time

Smart Guide™ to
Profiting from Mutual
Funds

Smart Guide™ to
Relieving Stress

Smart Guide™ to
Starting a Small Business

Smart Guide™ to
Vitamins and Healing
Supplements

Available soon:

Smart Guide™ to
Healing Back Pain

Smart Guide™ to
Maximizing Your
401(k) Plan

Smart Guide™ to
Planning for Retirement

Smart Guide™ to
Planning Your Estate

Smart Guide™ to
Sports Medicine

Smart Guide™ to
Yoga